THE REFERENCE SHELF   VOLUME 46 NUMBER 4

THE PRESIDENT
AND
THE CONSTITUTION

EDITED BY
GEORGE A. NIKOLAIEFF

THE H. W. WILSON COMPANY
NEW YORK   1974

THE REFERENCE SHELF

The books in this series contain reprints of articles, excerpts from books, and addresses on current issues and social trends in the United States and other countries. There are six separately bound numbers in each volume, all of which are generally published in the same calendar year. One number is a collection of recent speeches; each of the others is devoted to a single subject and gives background information and discussion from various points of view, concluding with a comprehensive bibliography. Books in the series may be purchased individually or on subscription.

Library of Congress Cataloging in Publication Data

Nikolaieff, George A   comp.
  The President and the Constitution.

  (The Reference shelf, v. 46, no. 4)
  Bibliography: p.
  1. Executive power--United States--Addresses, essays,
lectures. 2. Watergate Affair, 1972-   --Addresses,
essays, lectures. 3. Nixon, Richard Milhous, 1913-
--Impeachment--Addresses, essays, lectures. I. Title.
II. Series.
KF5053.A2N54   342'.73'062   74-16442
ISBN 0-8242-0523-5

PREFACE

One of the great qualities of the Constitution of the United States is that it provides us with safeguards for our democracy—a democracy in which the people do, in fact, have the ultimate power. It does so by dividing Federal power into three segments. These are, of course, the executive branch, the legislative branch, and the judiciary. This process of division distributes available power, thereby preventing any one branch from grasping full control.

But the Constitution goes one step further. To make certain that no single one of these branches of Federal power gets too strong, it provides a system of "checks and balances." In effect, they are a series of restraints that the several branches can place on one another. The concept of checks and balances is one that almost every school child is familiar with. Americans consider it a cornerstone of the entire American way of life and government. And so they are happy to sing its praises whenever the occasion arises.

This is ironic. The system of checks and balances implies that all three branches of Federal power are more or less equal; in fact, however, they are far from equal. Today, the presidency is the most powerful elective office in the world.

There is no sinister reason for this, in Washington at any rate. In the Executive, only the President need make up his mind before a decision is made and action taken accordingly. In Congress, on the other hand, more than four hundred Representatives and a hundred Senators, each with his own highly individual point of view, get involved in decision making.

In a fast-paced, technical world such as ours many gov-

ernment decisions must be made quickly. And since the
President is the natural one to make a decision, he frequently does. So, increasingly, power flows to him. Most
people in and out of government see the logic of this train
of events. At the same time, however, they cannot help but
remember that the system of checks and balances is supposed to keep the three branches of government roughly
equal. As the President grows stronger, they have an uncom-
fortable feeling of resentment and foreboding. And nowhere are those feelings more pronounced than in Congress
—the branch at whose expense the presidency has been
gaining its power.

It is a baffling situation without precedent. Consider,
for example, war powers. As Commander in Chief, the
President is responsible for the defense of our nation—
whether that means a threat from Cuba to Florida's coast
or one by Mainland China to an ally such as the Republic
of China on Taiwan. Congress, on the other hand, is specifically entrusted by the Constitution to declare war. Who
is right and who is wrong, then, when the President orders
air raids against enemy positions—enemy positions that are
not in Vietnam where soldiers are fighting, but in the
neighboring jungles where the enemy has its staging areas?

These are legitimate questions about presidential power,
about congressional power, and about the constitutional
basis for either side's arguments. And such questions (not
just in the area of defense but in many others as well) have
created an atmosphere of rivalry and tension between the
Congress and the executive branch.

To this fundamental set of premises one must add yet
another—the element of personality. Government, after all,
involves politics. And much of politics pivots on the skill
and personal traits, especially the desire for power, of its
main characters.

When he was President, Richard M. Nixon had a tendency to be secretive, distant, and moody. Unlike his prede-

cessors, he tended to act on his own without the appropriate gestures toward Congress that allow it to save face before the public. As one politician put it, "At least [President] Lyndon Johnson used to fly [congressional] committee chairmen down to his ranch to tell them he wasn't going to consult them on something. Nixon doesn't even bother."

It was against this background of mutual wariness that the Watergate scandal broke. Watergate has come to mean a whole series of questionable acts by the Executive. Which questionable action came first, which had the most damaging effect, are things people will ponder for decades to come. What is certain is that Watergate ignited the hostilities that had long been smoldering between Congress and the Executive and brought them to a confrontation, a confrontation that the judicial branch had to resolve.

This book comes on the heels of the dramatic ending to that confrontation. Within the span of less than a month three events took place. The Supreme Court ruled on executive privilege, saying President Nixon had to give up the tape recordings of certain conversations he had held in his White House office. Barely a week later the House Judiciary committee voted the first of three articles of impeachment. Shortly after that Mr. Nixon made public three of the taped conversations that the Court had ruled on. The evidence on those tapes proved so damaging that a Senate trial would almost certainly have ended in conviction. And so, rather than continue his own and the nation's agony, Richard Nixon resigned.

Mr. Nixon is the first President in our nation's history to resign. The constitutional conflict, the testing of the system of checks and balances, that too is without precedent. To fully understand it, it is necessary to examine some of the key conflicts—both short term and long—that brought on these extraordinary events.

The first section of this book deals with the point of no return, the moment in late October of 1973 when it became clear that we could not forget Watergate and go back to business as usual. President Nixon had just fired Archibald Cox, the special prosecutor on the Watergate break-in. That dismissal and the events and uproar that followed came to be known as "The Saturday Night Massacre." The important fact is that the action was taken to mean that President Nixon had, in effect, broken a promise to Congress that he would not interfere with the prosecutor's investigation. Moreover, the Nixon act implied he was concealing something.

Section II deals with the immediate reasons for the resounding hostility—Watergate. It reports what acts took place and the following acts that laid the groundwork for this crisis in our history.

In the third section we look at the modern presidency, its tendency to accumulate power even without asking for it, its ability to dominate the news media without effort and thus command the nation's attention. At the same time we look at a Congress that has been weakened, a Congress with a questionable will to fight.

The book's fourth section deals with the question of war powers. The President is the nation's Commander in Chief. He is responsible for our armed forces and hence our safety. Congress, on the other hand, is the only arm of government authorized by the Constitution to declare war. Because this is the most important area of conflict between the two branches, it is also the one on which the most decisive actions were taken.

Section V takes a close look at two of the three constitutional issues that the two opposing sides came to grips over: executive privilege and the President's refusal to spend money that the Congress had voted. To be able to do his work, a President must be immune from daily, petty annoyances. After all, he is the nation's leader. But how invulnerable should he be? How far should his privileges extend? Clearly the Congress and Richard Nixon had differing ideas.

The sixth section of the book looks at the ponderous machinery of Congress as it geared up for the impeachment proceedings. There are precedents in this area. And the Congress had a vast array of resources to draw on. But that does not mean the President was helpless. He could and did command the news media to his advantage. Through them he took his case directly to the people.

Whether or not his efforts did him any good becomes somewhat beside the point. For while he was working on his image, both Congress and the judicial branch exercised their unique authority under the Constitution: impeachment proceedings in Congress; and a legal review of executive privilege in the Supreme Court.

The seventh and final section of the book examines these momentous events: the Supreme Court's ruling, the fateful vote to impeach, the transfer of power and its dramatic finale. The conclusion is that the United States Constitution is alive and well and doing the job our forebears had intended for it—that is, preserving democracy.

The author would like to thank the publishers and authors of the material included in this compilation for their gracious consent to reprint it. Special thanks go to his family—Peter, Greg, and Rosalind—for their help and encouragement in making this compilation a reality.

GEORGE A. NIKOLAIEFF

September 1974

CONTENTS

IV. WAR POWERS

V. EXECUTIVE PRIVILEGE AND IMPOUNDMENT

VI. IMPEACHMENT STEPS BEGIN

VII. A President Resigns

I. THE DEMAND FOR IMPEACHMENT OR RESIGNATION

EDITOR'S INTRODUCTION

For weeks in late spring and summer of 1973 the Watergate committee, headed by North Carolina's Democratic Senator Sam Ervin, had dug into the incredible morass of deeds and misdeeds surrounding the 1972 presidential election. The material it was unearthing was fantastic and fascinating. John Dean 3d, a former counsel to the President, told them that President Nixon knew of a break-in at the Democratic National Committee headquarters and had sought to cover it up.

But as the summer wore into early fall public interest began to flag. Indeed, people noticed a perceptible backlash against the Watergate committee. There was a feeling that perhaps the President was being hounded too much. Then, in a rapid-fire series of events, things changed. The President was asked to provide tapes of conversations that could prove who was telling the truth. (Tapes had been made of almost all conversations in the President's office.)

At first the President refused. Later he consented. And only then was it revealed that two key tapes were simply missing. Next, in a move that shocked the nation, Mr. Nixon fired Archibald Cox. Mr. Cox was a law professor from Harvard whom Mr. Nixon had appointed to investigate Watergate events. In a highly independent fashion, Mr. Cox had proceeded to demand that Mr. Nixon (his boss, in effect) hand over more of the tapes made in his office. Furious, Mr. Nixon fired him. In the process, he had to accept the resignation of Elliot Richardson, his attorney general, who at his confirmation hearings, had told Congress he would not interfere with Cox's work.

Public reaction to these acts was so strong that it altered the nation's sentiments about impeachment. Impeachment is a formidable and difficult process; one way or another people shy away from the whole issue. But now, suddenly, impeachment was on everybody's mind. The opening article from the New York *Times* details this change of mood and how it came about.

The second selection, from the *Nation*, urges impeachment as the only viable procedure to resolve the issues that are perplexing the nation.

The third article, from the New York *Times*, lists some of the items that form the basis for charges against the President. At this stage they were only allegations, allegations that would later be weighed by the House Judiciary committee in its deliberations of whether or not to bring impeachment charges against Mr. Nixon. But even so they give a clear indication of why the President's popularity had fallen sharply. And they provide a clue to the degree of anger directed toward the White House.

THE SUDDEN MOOD FOR IMPEACHMENT [1]

The White House had sought to head it off. The Congress had cringed from it. But . . . [in mid-October 1973] the constitutional confrontation which had been threatening for months suddenly exploded in the first serious venture to impeach a President of the United States in 105 years.

The immediate cause was the Watergate tapes case. Its culmination wrought havoc in the Nixon Administration and provoked outrage in the electorate. President Nixon defied and then capitulated to the Federal courts. He dissolved the office of Watergate special prosecutor, then yielded to urgent demands of his party's leaders to recreate it. He pledged a free hand to the investigators of his own conduct, then circumscribed their independence. . . .

[1] From "Suddenly, Impeachment Is the Big, Open Issue," article by James M. Naughton, of the New York *Times* Washington Bureau. New York *Times.* p E 1. O. 28, '73. © 1973 by The New York Times Company. Reprinted by permission.

As members of Congress, stirred by an anguished and angry public, launched a formal inquiry into Mr. Nixon's conduct in office, they traced their concerns to events and attitudes spanning the President's five years in office: the secret bombing of Cambodia; the short-lived White House plan to burglarize and eavesdrop on domestic dissidents; the settlement of antitrust cases against the International Telephone and Telegraph Company; the grain sale to the Soviet Union; the dairy industry's cash contributions to the President's reelection campaign and blatant request for a quid pro quo; the still not fully explained financing of Mr. Nixon's California and Florida estates; the refusal by the White House to allocate funds appropriated by Congress; the dismissal . . . of the Watergate special prosecutor, Archibald Cox, and the method by which it was accomplished.

Those were but some of the matters cited as grounds for invoking the constitutional sanction against a President—impeachment in the House, trial by the Senate and either acquittal, or dismissal from office. The end result was far off. But the seriousness with which the process was begun was demonstrated by the volume and velocity of the demands for action by Congress. On . . . [one day] alone, Democrats in the House introduced eight resolutions of impeachment, one censure motion and thirteen proposals for formal investigations, while Republicans joined in sponsoring eight bills to remove the prosecution of the Nixon Administration from control of the White House.

The Attack

At a White House news conference . . . , Mr. Nixon attributed the plummeting confidence in his Administration to "outrageous, vicious, distorted reporting" by the television networks. Yet even his performance as he answered questions for thirty-eight minutes seemed to heighten awareness that his emotional health had become an open topic of public debate. He bore no ill will toward television newsmen, Mr. Nixon said with a grin, because "one can only be angry with those he respects." His Key Biscayne banker-friend C. G. Rebozo had shown "good judgment," Mr. Nixon explained, by accepting a secret $100,000 political gift from Howard Hughes, locking it in a vault for three years and returning it.

"The tougher it gets, the cooler I get," the President asserted. "Even in this week when many thought that the President was shellshocked, unable to act, the President acted decisively." (He put United States military forces on worldwide alert in a Middle East face-off with the Soviet Union.) "And I can assure you that whatever shocks gentlemen of the press may have, or others—political people—these shocks will not affect me and my doing my job," Mr. Nixon added.

One had to go no farther than the Western Union offices at the Capitol—where there was an unprecedented cascade of more than 250,000 telegrams . . . nearly all of them urging Mr. Nixon's impeachment—to find the abundant symptoms of national skepticism and bewilderment. And the events of the . . . nine days [following October 19] appeared to demand and defy explanation.

The "Compromise"

Ever since the burglary of Democratic party headquarters at the Watergate complex sixteen months ago, the White House had sought to avert a political crisis. Ironically, the containment of the situation appeared to have collapsed as a direct consequence of Mr. Nixon's proposal . . . to "compromise" the issue of the secret White House recordings of Watergate conversations.

Late . . . [on the day of] the deadline for White House compliance with a Federal appeals court order to turn over nine of the tapes to District Judge John J. Sirica, the President announced that he would neither obey the order nor appeal it to the Supreme Court. Instead, he offered to give Judge Sirica and the Senate Watergate committee White House summaries of the contents of the tapes, authenticated by Senator John C. Stennis, a Mississippi Democrat with an unsurpassed reputation for probity, but also a record of support for Mr. Nixon in his Watergate troubles.

Senators Sam J. Ervin Jr. and Howard H. Baker Jr., the Democratic chairman and ranking Republican on the Watergate committee, agreed. But Mr. Cox immediately said, "No." . . .

In a televised news conference Mr. Cox pictured the President's "compromise" as a way to undermine the Watergate prosecution and cover up other serious matters under investigation. A summary of the tape recordings would not likely be admissible as evidence in criminal trials, Mr. Cox said.

Mr. Cox also noted a condition of the President's proposal that became a major issue: the prosecutor had to agree "not to use the judicial process" to obtain a number of White House documents, some of which the President had already refused to provide, that might be relevant to the investigations. Mr. Cox made clear he would seek to have the President held in contempt of court.

At 8:24 P.M. . . . [October 20], the White House disclosed the bitter harvest of the "compromise": Attorney General Elliot L. Richardson, whose confirmation by the Senate had been conditioned on a pledge of an unhindered Cox investigation, resigned rather than carry out a presidential directive to fire Mr. Cox and abolish the special prosecutor's office. Deputy Attorney General William D. Ruckelshaus also refused to comply with Mr. Nixon's order and was dismissed as he prepared his letter of resignation. Solicitor General Robert H. Bork became Acting Attorney General and accorded to the President's order.

Mr. Cox and his staff were thought to have been investigating the $100,000 transaction between Mr. Rebozo and Howard Hughes. He was seeking voluminous notes kept by John D. Ehrlichman, one of the White House aides whose departure was forced by Watergate, and the special prosecutor was after a memo reportedly dictated by the

President after one discussion of the case in April. He was exploring large cash political donations made two years before the 1972 campaign and he said that he was looking into "possible abuses" of national security and other government agencies, including the Internal Revenue Service.

There had been television and press reports recently that Mr. Cox had begun investigating the possibility that large amounts of cash from wealthy men had been put into some kind of fund and managed for Mr. Nixon's benefit while he has been in the White House. When Mr. Nixon first ran for the vice presidency, it was disclosed that businessmen in California had provided a fund for his benefit. More than one citizen echoed the judgment of a man at a bar in Boston who said Mr. Cox had been sacked because he "got too close to home."

. . . [On October 21] congressional leaders began skimming through a 718-page research document published on October 9 by the House Judiciary committee. It was titled, *Impeachment.*

The Furor

The same day, White House officials privately offered assurance that there was little likelihood Congress would institute formal impeachment proceedings. To many in Washington, it seemed an accurate assessment.

But . . . [only two days later] Presidential Aide Alexander Haig and Charles Alan Wright, the President's special consultant on Watergate legal matters, would acknowledge that the White House had "miscalculated" the political effect of what Mr. Wright called "an extraordinarily generous proposal." It may have been a monumental understatement.

The nine hundred delegates to the biennial convention of the AFL-CIO stood up and cheered in Bal Harbour, Florida as they voted to demand Mr. Nixon's resignation or his impeachment if he refused to resign. One poll showed that 44 percent of those interviewed favored the President's impeachment.

Senators Ervin and Baker disclosed that they had not been told that Mr. Cox's dismissal and the dissolution of his office would follow his refusal to accept the tapes proposal. Former Attorney General Richardson endorsed Mr. Cox's course of action and publicly disputed the President's assertion that the compromise had been engineered by Mr. Richardson in the first place. What he had proposed, Mr. Richardson made clear, was a plan to turn over a laundered version of the tapes transcripts, not a summary, and he could not accept the restrictions on Mr. Cox's bid for future access to other tapes or documents.

Furthermore, at a news conference in the Great Hall of the Department of Justice, where career employees gave him a sustained ovation, Mr. Richardson confirmed . . . that the White House had discussed the dismissal of Mr. Cox days before it occurred as a way to "moot" the court battle over the tapes.

Judge Sirica convened his court . . . , expecting to receive formally the White House argument—submitted privately a day earlier—that the President's plan to produce a summary of the conversations would satisfy Judge Sirica and the United States Court of Appeals for the District of Columbia circuit.

The courtroom was jammed but so quiet that the swirls of reporters writing notes seemed magnified when the bailiff ordered everyone to rise at 2:08 P.M. and Judge Sirica entered, his face set in the somber mien of a man about to cite a President for contempt.

Judge Sirica looked at Mr. Wright and asked if the White House was prepared to file a response.

"May it please the court," the tall University of Texas law professor replied, "I am not prepared at this time to file a response. I am, however, authorized to say that the President of the United States would comply in all respects with the order of August 29 as modified by the order of the Court of Appeals."

As the 170 spectators drew in their breaths and Judge Sirica allowed himself a brief smile, Mr. Wright withdrew the White House compromise plan and said that, even if the court had accepted it, the "events of the weekend" had made it evident that there would be "those who would have said the President is defying the law." As much to the nation as to the court, Mr. Wright added: "This President does not defy the law."

Mr. Nixon, who had insisted since the existence of the tapes was revealed on July 16 that he never would give them up and thereby violate the "principle of confidentiality" in the White House, had agreed to give them up.

The Inquiry

Members of the House of Representatives, whose tenure depends on the biennial grace of the voters, do not often lead but nearly always follow pronounced public opinion. One after another, Republicans and Democrats alike reported the impact of Mr. Nixon's dismissal of Archibald Cox in staggering dimensions. Messages running 10 to 1 for impeachment, some said. Others described it as 50 to 1, a few at more than 100 to 1. No one could recall anything so lopsided, or so swift.

House Speaker Carl Albert, an Oklahoma Democrat who is constitutionally in line to succeed Mr. Nixon until Congress confirms the nomination of Gerald R. Ford, the House Republican leader, to succeed Spiro Agnew as Vice President, would not even entertain a reporter's questions about impeachment early this year. . . . [At this point] however, he and other House Democratic leaders agreed that the issue had to be referred to the Judiciary committee for consideration, and the Republican leaders, Mr. Ford among them, agreed. . . .

The twenty-one Democrats in control of the House Judiciary committee agreed unanimously to undertake what the chairman, Peter W. Rodino Jr. of New Jersey, called a "broad-scale" inquiry "similar to a grand jury" proceeding. The seventeen Republican members of the panel complained that the Democrats' plans to assemble a separate impeachment staff and give Mr. Rodino unlimited subpoena power smacked of partisanship and a "fishing expedition." But Vice-President-designate Ford said the inquiry should proceed.

What Next?

House Democrats scheduled quick action, beginning with a hearing . . . [October 29], on bills to create a prosecutor's office, independent of the White House. The most likely method was to enact a law giving Judge Sirica control over the investigation. A similar measure was introduced . . . [earlier] in the Senate with 53 of the 100 members as cosponsors. But Republican leaders, trying to salvage something out of the uproar, finally persuaded Mr. Nixon . . . , with the help of acting Attorney General Bork, to name an Administration successor to Mr. Cox.

Mr. Nixon announced at his news conference that Mr. Bork would designate the new prosecutor . . . [before the week was out]. The President said Mr. Cox's replacement would have "independence" and "total cooperation from the executive branch," virtually the same guarantee given the man he dismissed a week earlier. . . .

The one point on which there appeared to be universal agreement was contained in Mr. Nixon's comment . . . [October 27]: "It's time for those who are guilty to be prosecuted and for those who are innocent to be cleared."

RESIGNATION OR IMPEACHMENT? [2]

Much time can be wasted speculating about the two missing tapes. It is conceivable (anything is conceivable in Washington today) that they never existed. But there can be no doubt that two conversations—with Mitchell on June 20, 1972, and John Dean on April 15, 1973—were the

[2] From editorial "The Clamor for Resignation." *Nation.* 217:514-15. N. 19, '73. Reprinted by permission.

critically important ones. Nor can there be any doubt that, as early as September 29, the President knew that tapes of these conversations were either missing or nonexistent. Yet he concealed this fact from Senators Stennis, Ervin and Baker. He concealed it from the public. He concealed it from the press (if he had responded fully to one question at his October 26th press conference he would have disclosed the fact that these tapes were not available). And he also concealed the fact that they were missing in his initial overtures to Judge Sirica. Finally, it now appears that he even failed to tell his own counsel, Charles Alan Wright, that the two most vital tapes demanded by the judge would not be forthcoming.

Such conduct is inexcusable; it has destroyed any vestige of credibility that the President still retained. To Senator Goldwater, the President's credibility "has reached an all-time low from which he may not be able to recover." Similar sentiments have been voiced by Senators Pearson, Hatfield, Schweicker and Buckley, among other Republicans. Business leaders are deeply troubled and unhappy. Editorials urging the President to resign have appeared in the New York *Times, Time* (the first editorial in the fifty years of its existence), the Detroit *News,* the Denver *Post,* the Atlanta *Journal.* Republican Senator Edward Brooke has called for the President's resignation. So has columnist Joseph Alsop—a significant weather vane—and commentator Howard K. Smith. Senator Goldwater, "on vacation" in Wichita, Kansas—perhaps the first person in living memory to spend a vacation in Wichita—met with columnist William Buckley at the airport, and the latter then suggested that perhaps Nixon should resign. In fact something like a consensus is now emerging from former Nixon partisans—some of whom quietly, some publicly, are joining the movement to force the President out.

This mounting clamor should be viewed with a cold eye. Some months back resignation seemed to be the neatest, quickest and least traumatic way out of an impossible situation (see editorial, "The Case for Resignation," *Nation*, June 4). But with Agnew's resignation, the Ford nomination, the ouster of Cox, Richardson and Ruckelshaus, the deception about the tapes and other recent developments, the top priority is to get the impeachment inquiry under way. If Nixon had named as Vice President a person who had the qualities needed in a President—someone the public could view in that light—the case for resignation would have been more persuasive. But Ford was named not because he possessed these qualities but because he lacked them; it was assumed that he could win early confirmation and that his presence in the wings might discourage impeachment. The impeachment inquiry, if it is properly pressed, should resolve once and for all issues that have sorely perplexed and divided the nation. The people should *know* the facts; they are entitled to them. Impeachment offers the only constitutional means by which the case against the President can be made in an orderly public manner. If the President simply bows out now, the deeds which resulted in the initiation of the impeachment inquiry will never come to light. In retirement Nixon would sulk, plot and contend that "enemies" had stabbed him in the back. And if he is innocent, as he insists, he should in fairness be given an early opportunity to prove it, and the only available forum is the Senate sitting as an inquest of the nation.

And resignation now would have other consequences. It would lead to loudly orchestrated pleas for "healing" and "reconciliation," under cover of which the public would be encouraged to forget Watergate. Naturally, the Republicans would like Nixon to go, so that they could campaign in 1974 and 1976 free of the onus of defending him. Conservative Republicans of the Goldwater-Buckley type want to be rid of him because their "cause" has suffered recently a series of blows from which it may not recover. This cause nearly collapsed with Agnew's resignation. If

Nixon were on trial before the Senate the Conservatives would be forced to rally to his defense. . . .

If the President should resign, we would not weep; it is the clamor for resignation, and the possible consequences, that we find disturbing. In the perspective of recent events, resignation might lead to a national cop-out. If he departs voluntarily, ministers, editorial writers, opinion leaders and network commentators will rejoice that Watergate is now happily behind us; they will say that the crisis has been resolved, the nation "cleaned" and "purified" and that the time has now come for all good men to uphold the hand of President Ford. We would be told *ad nauseam* that Richard Nixon should be permitted to depart in peace to whichever coastal retreat he prefers and that nothing became his holding of the Office of President as well as his decision to leave it.

This Niagara of false sentiment would create an atmosphere in which the Watergate investigations and trials would be submerged. It would be "back to normalcy," with Gerald Ford as the historical counterpart of Calvin Coolidge. Faced with such prospects, the drumbeat for the President's resignation should not be permitted to slow down a systematic and careful impeachment inquiry. At the same time, the Ervin committee's term should be extended and a new independent prosecutor named by the courts and not by the President. Should Nixon linger on as a commuter President, dodging in and out of the White House, it would indeed be hazardous, but to permit the Watergate inquiries to go down the drain would be disastrous. It is far better that we face this crisis squarely and promptly than that we brush it aside and pretend that it never existed.

THE LIST OF POTENTIAL CHARGES [3]

A case can be made for the proposition that President Nixon should be held responsible for the activities of his

[3] From "A Catalogue of Matters Involving the President," article by David E. Rosenbaum, of the New York *Times* Washington Bureau. New York *Times.* p E 1. F. 10, '74. © 1974 by The New York Times Company. Reprinted by permission.

subordinates and that their crimes are in themselves bases for the President's impeachment. But a case can also be made for the opposite argument, and political reality makes it almost certain that if the House of Representatitives impeaches the President and if the Senate votes to remove him from office, it will be because of what Richard M. Nixon did himself.

That is why the inquiry under way in the House Judiciary committee will most likely end up concentrating on direct charges against the President. The chief counsel of that inquiry, John M. Doar, has divided his investigation into six broad categories: the Watergate burglary and its cover-up; the misuse of Government agencies and illegal campaign contributions; domestic surveillance; campaign intelligence activities; the President's personal finances; and excessive claims of presidential power.

What follows is a catalog of the principal allegations that have been made in the last year and a half against the President personally in each of these categories, except for campaign intelligence activities in which there is no direct allegation, and the President's public response.

Watergate and Cover-Up

Item: That the President, within days of the Watergate burglary, instructed his top aides to order the Central Intelligence Agency to block the Federal Bureau of Investigation's inquiry. The initial investigation of the burglary was thus held up for at least two weeks.

Response: Mr. Nixon has acknowledged having tried to limit the FBI investigation because he believed, "incorrectly," that "an unrestricted investigation of Watergate might lead to and expose covert national security operations."

Item: That the President sanctioned his aides' efforts to hide the facts about the burglary for six months. John W. Dean 3d, who was White House counsel, told the Senate Watergate committee and, presumably, the prosecutors that Mr. Nixon knew of the Watergate cover-up as early as September 1972, that he was aware of the payment of "hush money" to the Watergate defendants and that he discussed executive clemency for the defendants with his principal aides. These points, which could amount to felonies, have not been corroborated by other public witnesses.

Response: The White House contends that Mr. Dean was lying. President Nixon has said that he first learned the extent of the cover-up on March 21, 1973, and that he immediately "personally ordered those conducting the investigations to get all the facts and to report them directly to me." All major public witnesses have denied that such orders were given to them.

Item: That the President tried repeatedly to strangle the investigation by the special prosecutor. For several months, Mr. Nixon jealously guarded the tapes of his White House conversations and other evidence and challenged in court the prosecutor's right to subpoena them. After the Court of Appeals ruled against him, the President proposed what he called a compromise. When the former special prosecutor, Archibald Cox, refused to accept the compromise, Mr. Nixon ordered him dismissed, an action that a district court subsequently (but academically) found to be illegal. The new special prosecutor, Leon Jaworski, said . . . that, while the White House had turned over some evidence after he specifically asked for it, other tapes and documents were still being withheld.

Response: Mr. Nixon has contended time and again that, to protect his office, certain communications between the President and his foremost aides must remain confidential.

Item: That the President was responsible for the destruction of evidence. In a letter to Senator Sam J. Ervin Jr. last July 23, Mr. Nixon said that the Watergate tapes were "under my sole personal control [and] will remain so." Four months later, it was disclosed that $18\frac{1}{2}$ minutes of conversation on a crucial tape had been obliterated. . . . [In January 1974] technical experts reported that the obliteration had been caused by a manual erasure, and the implication was that it had been done intentionally.

Response: The White House has said only that Mr. Nixon did not erase the tape personally and does not know how it happened.

The Agencies

Item: That the President promoted governmental action against his political enemies. Mr. Dean testified that Mr. Nixon had ordered the compilation of the names of political opponents of the Administration with the aim of having the Internal Revenue Service harass them after the 1972 election. Such lists were made, but there is little public evidence that the IRS actually took action against those on the lists.

Response: The White House has said that the lists were kept to assure that opponents were not invited to social functions or given other favors.

Item: That the President granted favors to milk producers in return for campaign contributions. Following a 1970 pledge from the dairy industry in a letter to the President of $2 million in campaign contributions, Mr. Nixon imposed quotas on the importation of certain dairy products. The next year, the Agriculture department reversed a decision against raising milk price supports shortly after leading milk producers had met with Mr. Nixon. Dairy cooperatives eventually contributed $427,500 to the Nixon campaign.

Response: The White House, in a statement last month [January 1974], said that the imposition of quotas was based on recommendations by the Tariff Commission. It was acknowledged that "political considerations" (such as the need to gain favor in the farm states) influenced the increase in price supports, but it was contended that campaign donations were not considered when the decision was made.

Item: That the President ordered the favorable settlement of an antitrust suit against the International Telephone and Telegraph Company in return for a campaign donation. Former Attorney General Richard G. Kleindienst said . . . [in the fall of 1973] that Mr. Nixon had called him in 1971 and, with no discussion, had ordered him to drop antitrust proceedings against ITT. Charles W. Colson, former special counsel to the President, said in a memorandum that Senate hearings on the ITT affair could "lay this case on the President's doorstep." The company once pledged up to $400,000 to help finance the 1972 Republican National Convention.

Response: In its statement . . . [in January 1974] the White House said that Mr. Nixon had ordered Mr. Kleindienst to drop the suits solely because he disagreed with the philosophy on which the suits were based—that "bigness per se" is bad.

Item: That the President accepted a secret contribution from Howard Hughes, one of the world's richest men, in 1968. Mr. Nixon is said to have discussed with Richard Danner, then a campaign aide, the possibility of a Hughes donation. Later, Mr. Danner went to work for Mr. Hughes and delivered $100,000 in hundred-dollar bills to the President's closest friend, Bebe Rebozo. Three years later, Mr. Rebozo returned the money. He said he had kept it in a safe deposit box. Mr. Nixon met with Mr. Danner at about the time part of the money was delivered to Mr. Rebozo and shortly before it was all returned. Some investigators believe there is a connection between the donation and the Administration's decision to permit Hughes interests to buy a Las Vegas casino.

Response: Mr. Nixon has said that he did not know of the $100,000 until after the election, despite the fact that Mr. Rebozo was his frequent companion. The donation was not discussed at the President's meetings with Mr. Danner, according to the White House.

Surveillance

Item: That the President created a secret police force. Mr. Nixon has acknowledged having ordered the creation of the special White House unit known as the Plumbers, whose job it was to plug leaks of information to the press. This unit was responsible for the burglary of the office of Dr. Daniel Ellsberg's former psychiatrist in 1971.

Response: The plumbers were created, Mr. Nixon has said, because leaks of national security information, including the Pentagon Papers, were "a threat so grave as to require extraordinary action." Mr. Nixon said he did not know ahead of time about the planned burglary of the psychiatrist's office and would have disapproved it had he known.

Item: That the President withheld from authorities information about the burglary of the psychiatrist's office for thirty-nine days before he allowed it to be reported to the court where Dr. Ellsberg was on trial. After the disclosure last May [1973], the charges against Dr. Ellsberg were dismissed.

Response: In his August 15, 1973, statement, Mr. Nixon said that, since no information was obtained in the burglary and since it was critical to keep secret the other activities of the plumbers, he decided initially to withhold evidence about the burglary and to prevent the Justice department from investigating the case. On the advice of Mr. Kleindienst, he said, he released the information.

Item: That the President tried to bribe the judge in the Ellsberg trial. Between the time Mr. Nixon learned of the burglary of the psychiatrist's office and the time the information was given to the court, the White House, with the President's knowledge, asked Judge W. Matthew Byrne Jr. if he would be interested in the FBI directorship.

Response: Mr. Nixon, at a news conference in August [1973], said that Judge Byrne had been sounded out about the position because he was the "best man" for the job and that he had never discussed the Ellsberg case with the judge.

Item: That the President approved, in 1970, a far-reaching intelligence plan drafted by an aide, Tom Charles Huston, that included authorization for burglaries, wiretapping, mail covers and other illegal tactics. The President's approval was rescinded five days later after J. Edgar Hoover opposed the plan.

Response: The President has contended that the wave of bombings on college campuses and the lack of coordination among various Government intelligence agencies led him to approve the plan.

Item: That the President approved the wiretapping in 1969 of more than a dozen White House aides and newsmen.

Response: The taps were necessary, Mr. Nixon said . . . [in May 1973], "to tighten the security of highly sensitive material." The wiretaps were "legal at the time," Mr. Nixon said, apparently referring to the fact that it was not until 1972 that the Supreme Court declared such wiretapping without court warrants unconstitutional.

Item: That the President ordered the Secret Service to follow his brother and tap his brother's telephone, apparently in an effort to prevent F. Donald Nixon's relations with the Howard Hughes organization from becoming an embarrassment to the Nixon reelection campaign.

Response: The President has said that his brother knew of the surveillance and that it was done to protect him from persons, particularly foreign agents, who might try to get him to use "improper influence."

Personal Finances

Item: That the President did not pay proper Federal and state taxes. Mr. Nixon, during his presidency, has paid only nominal Federal income taxes because he took a huge deduction for the donation of his vice presidential papers to the National Archives and because he did not report a capital gain on the sale of California property. Presidential lawyers have conceded that the deed on the gift of the papers was backdated to show that the transaction took place before the law was changed to prohibit a deduction for such gifts. After he was elected President, Mr. Nixon sold his New York apartment and bought the house in San

Clemente, California. Claiming San Clemente as his principal residence, he did not pay Federal capital gains tax on his profit from the sale of the New York apartment. However, claiming the District of Columbia as his permanent residence, he has not paid state income taxes in California since he became President.

Response: Mr. Nixon has maintained that his accountants assured him he was complying with the law when he filed his Federal tax returns. He has pledged to pay additional taxes if either the IRS or the Joint Congressional Committee on Internal Revenue Taxation find that he owes money. The White House has said, and California authorities have agreed, that Mr. Nixon was not a California resident for state tax purposes.

Item: That the President used public funds to improve his private properties. Some $10 million in public funds has been spent on properties in California and Florida. Some of the money went for such improvements as landscaping, a swimming pool cleaner, a beach cabana and a shuffleboard court.

Response: Mr. Nixon has said that the Government expenditures were necessary for security reasons and that some of the work actually reduced the value of his property.

The Use of Power

Item: That the President ordered, without congressional authorization and without announcing it publicly, a bombing campaign in Cambodia in 1969 and 1970, and permitted operations in Laos in 1970 after Congress had enacted legislation prohibiting ground combat there.

Response: Mr. Nixon, in a speech last summer [1973] to the Veterans of Foreign Wars, said his actions were taken to protect American lives and that he would take the same actions again in similar circumstances.

Item: That the President impounded, or refused to spend, $40 billion that had been appropriated by Congress. Most of the money was intended for social problems.

Response: The White House has repeatedly argued that Congress was irresponsible in appropriating the money and that, since Congress was unsuccessful in balancing revenues and expenditures, the President had to do so himself.

II. THE WATERGATE SCANDAL

EDITOR'S INTRODUCTION

Today the term Watergate is used to encompass a full-blown scandal of many parts. There are questions of payoff; questions of breaking and entering; questions of political harassment, of taking campaign contributions illegally, of improper use of Government agencies.

It all began with an incredible incident. Five men were caught burglarizing the Democratic National Committee headquarters, which just happened to be located in Washington's Watergate, a residential and office building complex. From then on, with pressure from the press, the tempo of the investigation and revelations began to pick up speed.

Articles in this section seek to provide the chronology of events as Watergate built from an incident (presidential Press Secretary Ronald Ziegler called it a "third-rate burglary") into a constitutional crisis.

The first article, from *Senior Scholastic*, describes the nature of the crisis. The remaining articles focus on the different elements that kept prodding the investigators further and further along. The second article, for example, focuses on the press. Initially, it was the press (and most notably the Washington *Post*) that seized on the Watergate break-in as a possible sign that important forces were involved. Next, the Senate Select Committee, headed by Senator Sam Ervin, began to conduct hearings. Televised day after day, they provided one revelation after another. The third article is a summary of the facts and possibilities that the hearings brought to light before they recessed for the summer. (The committee reconvened in the fall. But

it was its findings in the first series of hearings that made
the principal impact.)

The fourth and last article in the section is *Time* magazine's story on its selection of the man of the year for 1973.
That man was John Sirica, the Federal judge overseeing
Watergate developments. In extraordinary moves he used
powers available to him as a judge in his attempt to uncover the truth of Watergate.

WATERGATE:
ONLY A "THIRD-RATE BURGLARY"? [1]

The time is 9:59 A.M. Everyone is in place. Around the
country millions of people focus their TV sets. Lights!
Camera! Action! The continuing saga of Watergate is on
the air.

For five months (with a summer break) the Senate
Watergate hearings, live from Washington, have been bur-
rowing deeper and deeper into the vast tangled web that
has made the word *Watergate* known throughout most of
the world.

The Senate Watergate investigating committee, chaired
by Senator Sam Ervin (Democrat, North Carolina), has heard
scores of witnesses. They have piled up huge stacks of testimony. And in the process they have made celebrities of
senators on one side of the witness table and those who came
to testify on the other. Republicans Howard Baker of Tennessee and Lowell Weicker of Connecticut have become
familiar faces in most parts of the nation. And the "old
country lawyer," as he calls himself, has made the name of
Senator Sam Ervin familiar everywhere.

The public itself has had a rare chance to take a look at
some of the men behind the scenes responsible for the day-
to-day Government policy that touches the lives of millions
of Americans. These include people like John Dean, H. R.

[1] From article entitled "Watergate . . . So What." *Senior Scholastic.* 103:4-9.
O. 18, '73. Reprinted by permission from *Senior Scholastic,* © 1973 by Scholastic
Magazines, Inc.

Haldeman, John Erlichman, and John Mitchell. Before the break-in at Democratic national headquarters in June of 1972, it would be a fair bet that hardly one American in a hundred had heard of these men—with the exception, perhaps of former United States Attorney General John Mitchell. Today Erlichman, Dean, and Haldeman are nearly as well known as the President.

The Break-In

It was a long time before people began to suspect that the Watergate affair might be more than just a botched-up job carried out by bungling burglars.

Watergate and everything that goes with it—ruined careers, indictments, jail sentences, and the talk of impeachment of President Nixon—all goes back to a spring evening at a luxury apartment and office complex hard by the Potomac River, in the northwest section of Washington.

A sharp-eyed guard named Frank Wills spotted a door whose lock had been taped to keep it open. He pulled off the tapes, called the police, and the Watergate dam burst.

The door led to offices of the Democratic national headquarters. Five men were caught inside the Democratic party offices in the act of burglary. They were arrested by the District of Columbia police, hauled off to jail, tried, and sentenced to terms in jail.

So much for that. Or so it seemed at the time. The act was described as "a third-rate burglary." Some people took it—criminal as it was—as a prank, or a joke in poor taste. Others asked themselves: "What possible connection could the President of the United States, or any member of the presidential team, have with such a sordid affair as that?"

"No one on the White House staff, no one in this Administration, presently employed, was involved" in the break-in, President Nixon announced.

But there were nagging doubts in the minds of some people. There were too many unanswered questions. Who were these burglars? For whom were they working? Where did they get all the crisp $100 bills found on them? They had electronic bugging equipment with them when they were caught. Who wanted the information those bugs would pick up?

Three of the burglars—Bernard Barker, Virgilio Gonzales, and Eugenio Martinez—were Cuban immigrants. It would later be learned that Barker had helped to set up the ill-fated American-sponsored invasion of Cuba in 1962. Another of the burglars was James McCord. McCord, it turned out, was the head of security for the Republican National Committee.

It was clear by now that this was no mere political prank. Someone in a position of authority in the Republican party had been caught red-handed breaking the law. But one question remained unanswered. Was this just a stupid stunt by a few over-eager, low-ranking people? Or did higher-ups know what was going on?

The Probe Begins

The break-in took place in June, about five months before the presidential election of November 1972 in which President Nixon, Republican, was reelected over George McGovern, the Democratic candidate. The Republican National Committee was aided in the campaign by a group called the Committee for the Re-election of the President.

But somehow it just didn't smell right. The pieces didn't fit. Perhaps the first clue that something was seriously wrong was when G. Gordon Liddy was fired by John Mitchell, head of the Committee for the Re-election of the President (CREEP), eleven days after the break-in. The FBI was sniffing into the burglary case. They wanted to know who else was involved in the caper, besides the men actually caught in Democratic headquarters. When they tried to question Liddy, a lawyer working for the President's re-election campaign, Liddy refused to talk.

Still, there was no hard evidence that anyone beyond the Watergate five had actualy broken the law. It was only later, largely through the investigation of two Washington *Post* reporters, Carl Bernstein and Bob Woodward, that more and more information about Watergate began to emerge from the mist.

The Washington *Post* began to carry daily stories by the pair of reporters that higher-ups in the Nixon Administration were involved in the planning of the Watergate bugging and break-in. Eventually, information about other campaign practices began to seep out.

Through it all, the White House continued to issue denials. The President, through his press spokesman Ronald Ziegler, accused the press of blowing up the Watergate affair out of all proportion. Ziegler specifically attacked the *Post* stories as "a political effort, character assassination, and the shoddiest type of journalism."

By the end of the summer of '72, however, it became clear that the bugging and burglary were only a preview of troubles to come. It was reported that the FBI had information that Nixon political campaigners had at least fifty special agents operating around the country whose job it was to sabotage and spy on the Democrats. It became clear that the burglary at the Democratic headquarters was only the tip of a very large iceberg.

Finally there was a call for an official Senate inquiry into the Watergate case. Senator Ervin agreed to head the committee. And the dramatic unfolding of layers of intrigue appeared on TV screens across America.

Witness after witness told of "dirty tricks," such as anonymous fake letters accusing Democratic candidates of sexual misconduct. One such letter charged that Senator Edmund Muskie (a presidential hopeful from Maine) had made an ethnic slur about Americans of French-Canadian descent. It cost the Senator considerable support. There was testimony about secret campaign funds illegally solicited without disclosure of the donor's name—as required by law. It was reported that a secret $700,000 fund existed to pay for sabotage and spying on Democratic rallies. The Administration denied the charge. Later they said there was such a fund, but that it was only around $300,000. Moreover, it was claimed, the fund was not to pay for illegal activity.

By midsummer of this year [1973], "Watergate" had become a word that referred to a whole range of illegal activity. Moreover, it was now a word which referred to a state of mind—not just the breaking and entering of an office. It was now a word that referred to people's ideas about politics, the presidency, and what is right and wrong in America. It refers as well to what has been called the "state of siege" mentality that was said to have created the whole thing in the first place.

Author Theodore White, in *The Making of the President 1972*, said he tried to locate the spot where the seeds of Watergate were first planted. He pointed to the so-called plumbers as the first clue to what was to come. This group was formed to find and plug "leaks" to the press and public of confidential and classified Government information.

The plumbers tapped the phones of several Administration officials, poked through private files, and broke into private offices. Their most famous operation was the break-in at the office of the psychiatrist of Daniel Ellsberg. Ellsberg had leaked to the press the secret Pentagon Papers that showed how the United States got involved in the Vietnam war.

"It is here," says White, "that the sense of horror at Watergate begins."

"National security," was given as the basic reason for the plumbers' missions. In one sense, the White House argued that it had to take extralegal measures to fight a threat to the national security.

Back in the late 1960s, demonstrations against the war in Vietnam became especially violent. There were scattered political bombings across the United States. In response to this threat, some in the Nixon Administration proposed the creation of a vast spying program aimed at the American public at large.

The program included such things as telephone taps and burglary. The program was almost enacted. But it was eventually killed because of the opposition of the late J. Edgar Hoover, director of the FBI. The CIA was also opposed to the idea, and rejected the Nixon Administration view that demonstrations were inspired and supported by foreign powers.

At any rate, it became clear throughout the months of the Senate hearings that some of this feeling about enemies in the land remained with some members of the White House staff and the Committee for the Re-election of the President. According to this view, the threat of subversion was real, and it was necessary to "fight fire with fire." "Radicals," they agree, were active in the Democratic presidential campaign. White House spokesmen said they feared violent demonstrations and assassination attempts during the presidential campaign.

President Is Accused

But two of the biggest bombshells of all came during the testimony of White House aides John Dean and Alexander Butterfield. Dean told a packed Senate hearing room that the President knew of attempts to cover up the Watergate scandal—and knew of attempts to prevent the scandal from leading to the White House staff. There was a vigorous denial of this from the White House. Those who followed the hearings wondered how it was possible to tell who was telling the truth.

Another bombshell came when White House aide Alexander Butterfield testified. Butterfield startled the committee when he disclosed that President Nixon had special tape recorders installed in three offices where he regularly worked. If Dean was right, talk about the cover-up would be recorded on tapes. Was the President telling the truth? Was Dean? The tapes, it was argued, would tell the full story.

If the world thought it had heard everything in the

Watergate case, it was in for a shock. The drama was to unfold even further. A Federal court judge, John Sirica, and a special prosecutor in the case, Archibald Cox, said that the tapes must be given up by the White House. The President refused. And one of the greatest constitutional battles of US history was on.

President Nixon insisted that the separation of powers allows him to keep private, confidential presidential information. This, he argued, would include tapes and other records. Some legal scholars disagreed. No man, including the President, has the right to make such a decision in a case in which he may be liable to prosecution. If the President did know about the burglary, or if he helped to cover it up afterward, they said, he is guilty of obstructing justice. And that is a crime. . . .

Through it all, some people have continued to ask: what's so bad about Watergate? Political pranks, they say, are part of American history. But Watergate, others argue, has turned out to be more than a prank. The President himself has condemned the Watergate affair.

"Practices of this kind do not represent what I believe government should be," said Nixon, "or what I believe politics should be. In a free society, the institutions of government belong to the people. They must never be used against the people."

THE INVESTIGATIVE REPORTERS [2]

After a year of enduring hot blasts from the Nixon Administration and chilling subpoenas from the courts, investigative reporters were riding high again . . . [in mid-May 1973]. The deep-diggers walked off (as they usually do) with the lion's share of the annual Pulitzer prizes. And at the second annual "A. J. Liebling Counter-Convention," a gathering of the working press in Washington, elation over the Watergate disclosures was so widespread that some news-

[2] From article entitled "Deep-Diggers Rampant." *Newsweek*. 21:60. My. 21, '73. Copyright Newsweek, Inc. 1973, reprinted by permission.

men began to warn their colleagues against patting themselves on the back.

To no one's surprise, the king of this year's muckrakers turned out to be The Washington *Post*, which won a Pulitzer for its Watergate investigation, conducted mainly by Carl Bernstein, twenty-nine, and Bob Woodward, thirty. In addition, Robert Boyd and Clark Hoyt of the Knight Newspapers won the national reporting award for uncovering Senator Thomas Eagleton's history of psychiatric treatment. The Chicago *Tribune* was honored for reporting on violations of primary-election law, and the Sun Newspapers of Omaha, a chain of weeklies, won a prize for one of the year's unlikeliest exposés: the revelation that Boys Town has a lot more money than most people thought.

Hubris

The Counter-Convention, as a result, produced some swaggering talk of professional vindication. "I've come to Washington," joked one reporter, "to receive my personal apology from the President." But despite the inevitable crowing, there were many stern warnings against journalistic *hubris.* . . .

Press critic Ben H. Bagdikian noted soberingly that "no more than fourteen reporters" of the 2,200 stationed in Washington had done substantial work on Watergate, and that relatively few publications had given the story all-out pursuit. In a column deploring his profession's "orgy of self-congratulation," Washington *Post* columnist David S. Broder (himself a Pulitzer Prize winner . . . [in 1973]) warned that "it would be prudent for us to view this wave of adulation with the same skepticism we direct toward other passing public fancies." And at the Counter-Convention itself (which was conceived as the rank and file's answer to earlier conclaves of editors and publishers), Bob Woodward told a cheering throng: "People are saying this is the finest hour for investigative journalism . . . but there's much more the press should have done, and so much more to do."

Rumor

Some critics—including people usually regarded as allies of liberal journalism—thought the press was doing too much already. Senate leaders Mike Mansfield and Hugh Scott protested the publication and leaks from the Watergate probes. Democratic Senator William Proxmire went so far as to accuse the press of using "McCarthyistic" tactics against the President. Said Proxmire: "The press is rapidly developing a reckless momentum of reporting innuendo and rumor in this Watergate case against President Nixon." He specifically denounced a story . . . which reported that former White House counsel John Dean had given investigators information that seemed to link Mr. Nixon indirectly to the Watergate cover-up. "I think fair is fair," protested Proxmire—despite the fact that, only the day before, he himself had told a friend privately that he believed President Nixon to be "involved in Watergate up to his ears."

Nonetheless, Proxmire's point was a good one: premature disclosures could indeed malign innocent parties and prejudice the case against guilty ones. But many observers echoed the equally valid question asked by James Reston of the New York *Times*: "Would this scandal have reached the present point of disclosure if the press had not reported the secret testimony of witnesses in this case?" Probably not, but there is still a right way and a wrong way to do investigative reporting. "We wrote perhaps two hundred stories in less than a year," Woodward recalled . . . [in May 1973], "and it was always one step forward at a time—and a very small step at that." The proper role of the investigative reporter, in short, is reckless disregard for everything—except caution.

THE COMMITTEE'S FINDINGS [3]

The huge bulk of the Watergate committee testimony contains so many diversions, evasions, conflicts and lies that the record of what has been learned is still unclear.

There is more to be heard. After a month-long recess Senator Sam Ervin's Select Committee still expects to question seven further witnesses about the Watergate burglary and the subsequent cover-up. Also missing from the record is the potentially (but not necessarily) decisive evidence from the tapes of conversations secretly recorded by the President. Nixon's latest account of the affair . . . could alter the weight of evidence already before the committee.

Yet the hearing recess provides a fitting opportunity for the Ervin committee staff to begin sifting the testimony in search of tentative conclusions—and perjury. *Time*, too, has assessed the evidence to date and, without attempting to indicate individual criminal culpability, offers this analysis:

The 1970 Intelligence Plan

Undisputed facts. President Nixon on July 23, 1970, notified four Federal intelligence-gathering agencies—the FBI, CIA, National Security Agency and Defense Intelligence Agency—that he had approved a new plan for the use of some previously banned tactics in gathering information on antiwar demonstrators, campus rioters, radical bomb throwers and black extremists. The tactics included breaking and entering, the opening of personal mail and the interception of communication between US residents and foreign points. One of the plan's originators, Nixon aide Tom Huston, pointed out in a memo that breaking and entering, at least, was "clearly illegal." The plan was opposed by FBI Director J. Edgar Hoover (for reasons not entirely clear, since the FBI has not been above breaking and entering in

[3] From "Watergate I: The Evidence to Date." *Time*. 8:16-18. Ag. 20, '73. Reprinted by permission from *Time*, the weekly newsmagazine; copyright Time Inc.

espionage cases); his objections were supported by Attorney General John Mitchell.

In dispute. Nixon said in his May 22 statement that because of Hoover's protests, he rescinded his approval of the plan five days after granting it. He said the plan never went into effect. Neither Mitchell nor John Dean, then White House counsel, could recall seeing orders canceling the plan. No such documents were produced. Questions by senators indicated some doubts about whether the plan had actually been promptly and completely killed.

Weight of evidence. The lack of any evidence that any illegal acts have been carried out by the intelligence agencies seems to indicate that the plan was indeed rescinded. Similar acts, however, were carried out by the White House plumbers.

What did Nixon know? However temporarily, he approved the plan—and thus approved acts that he had been advised would be illegal.

Creation of the Plumbers

Undisputed facts. Concerned about leaks of classified Government information to newspapers, especially the Pentagon Papers, Nixon in June 1971 created a White House group called the Special Investigations Unit, also known as the plumbers. It was supervised by John Erlichman, directed by Egil Krogh and included David Young, E. Howard Hunt and G. Gordon Liddy. Its activities included tapping the phones of officials and newsmen suspected of handling leaked information; burglarizing the office of a psychiatrist consulted by Pentagon Papers defendant Daniel Ellsberg; investigating Senator Edward Kennedy's Chappaquiddick accident; covertly spiriting ITT lobbyist Dita Beard out of Washington; and fabricating a State department cable linking the Kennedy Administration with the assassination of South Vietnam's President Diem. Two of the plumbers, Liddy and Hunt, later were convicted of wiretapping and burglary at the Watergate.

In dispute. The President's May 22 statement denied that the plumbers were assigned to do anything illegal. It said that their duties were strictly in the field of national security and, beyond plugging leaks, they were to compile "an accurate record of events related to the Vietnam war." Ehrlichman portrayed the plumbers' main purpose as to "stimulate various agencies and departments" in controlling leaks. He rejected suggestions by senators that the plumbers resembled a secret-police group or that their activity was primarily political.

Weight of evidence. The plumber operations described by Mitchell as "White House horrors," especially the fake Vietnam cable, the Dita Beard foray, and the Chappaquiddick probe, did not at all fit the Nixon or Ehrlichman descriptions of the plumbers' role. These acts were highly political and had nothing to do with national security.

What did Nixon know? No witness admitted discussing with Nixon any of these plumber activities except for the burglary of Ellsberg's psychiatrist's office. Yet Nixon created the plumbers to deal with a threat "so grave as to require extraordinary actions," and he described their work as "highly sensitive." There is a strong possibility that he kept informed of all plumber activities. If he did not, he should have.

The Ellsberg Burglary

Undisputed facts. Nixon on May 22 said he ordered the plumbers to examine Ellsberg's "associates and his motives" because no one knew "what additional national secrets Mr. Ellsberg might disclose." Directed by plumbers Hunt and Liddy, a team of burglars paid by the White House broke into the Los Angeles office of Dr. Lewis Fielding in September 1971, in a search for Ellsberg's psychiatric records. (White House aides Krogh and Young were aware of this burglary in advance.)

In dispute. Ehrlichman denied authorizing the burglary but admitted approving a memo from Krogh and Young suggesting that "a covert operation be undertaken to examine all the medical files still held by Ellsberg's psychiatrist." This information was needed, Ehrlichman said, not to prosecute Ellsberg (such evidence would be inadmissible) but to provide more data for a "psychological profile" that the plumbers had asked the CIA to compile; the White House had found the CIA's first such report inadequate. He rejected Senator Lowell Weicker's charge that the aim was to "smear" Ellsberg for political purposes.

Weight of evidence. Ehrlichman's admitted approval of a "covert operation" strongly suggests that he gave a go-ahead to the burglary; Young has told the Ervin committee staff that Ehrlichman in fact did so. A memo from Young to Ehrlichman just before the burglary said that "we have already started on a negative press image for Ellsberg" and that if the "present Hunt/Liddy project Number 1 is successful," there must a a "game plan" for its use. This suggests a move by the White House to smear Ellsberg.

What did Nixon know? Dean claims that Krogh told him the burglary orders came "right out of the Oval Office." Ehrlichman, curiously, argued that Nixon would have been within his legal rights in ordering such a burglary. Nixon said he "did not authorize and had no knowledge of any illegal means to be used" to assess Ellsberg's motives. He said he was informed by Attorney General Richard Kleindienst on April 25 that Hunt was involved in the burglary and promptly agreed that the Ellsberg trial judge, Matthew Byrne, must be informed. Yet a White House–supplied log of Nixon-Dean meetings indicates that Dean told Nixon about the burglary more than a month earlier, on March 17. If Nixon was not actually informed of all plumber activities, he was, in this case, remarkably slow in telling the judge.

Overtures to Judge Byrne

Undisputed facts. Shortly before the Ellsberg case was expected to go to the jury, Nixon told Ehrlichman to find out whether Judge Byrne would be interested in a possible appointment as FBI director. Ehrlichman twice met briefly in California with the judge to discuss this. Nixon also briefly met him.

In dispute. Ehrlichman claims that since no formal offer was made and the judge did not object to discussing the matter, the meetings were not improper. He said neither he nor the President intended to influence the Ellsberg case.

Weight of evidence. Any approach to a sitting judge by Government officials who have an obvious interest in wanting the Government's case to prevail is wholly improper. If a private citizen made a similar move, he could be prosecuted.

What did Nixon know? He ordered the contact made.

The Liddy Plans

Undisputed facts. After joining the Committee for the Re-election of the President, former plumber Liddy twice presented extravagant intelligence-gathering plans to Dean, Mitchell and Jeb Stuart Magruder, the Nixon committee deputy, while Mitchell was still Attorney General. The plans, which initially included wiretapping Nixon's Democratic opponents, using call girls to blackmail Democrats at their national convention, and the kidnapping of anti-Nixon radical leaders—all at a cost estimated at $1 million—were rejected each time by Mitchell. Scaled down to concentrate on the wiretapping, the plans were presented again by Magruder at a third meeting with Mitchell at Key Biscayne after Mitchell had resigned from the Justice department to head the Nixon committee. A Mitchell deputy, Fred LaRue, was present. Besides the Watergate, the wiretapping targets included Democratic convention headquarters at Miami Beach and the headquarters of the eventual Democratic nominee.

In dispute. Magruder claimed that Mitchell approved the plan at this third meeting. Mitchell claimed he bluntly rejected it. LaRue said he did neither, in his presence, but delayed a decision. Magruder also claimed that Charles Colson, a White House aide at the time, applied pressure on him to get the plan into motion. (Colson has admitted calling Magruder about Hunt's and Liddy's "security activities" but claimed he did not know what they were.) Magruder said he reported Mitchell's approval to Gordon Strachan, an assistant to H. R. Haldeman, so that Haldeman would be informed. Strachan said he included this item in a memo to Haldeman. Haldeman could not recall reading it. Dean said he reported the first two Liddy meetings to Haldeman; the latter said he did not remember this either.

Weight of evidence. An intelligence-gathering operation budgeted at $250,000 and involving such risky and illegal activities as burglary and wiretapping would not have been undertaken on Liddy's authority—especially if Mitchell had flatly rejected it. Nor did Magruder carry that kind of clout. The likelihood is that Mitchell did give some sign of approval. There may also have been White House pressure.

What did Nixon know? He has forcefully denied any knowledge of the Liddy plans. Dean said that he "assumed" that Haldeman had reported such significant information to the President, but that is highly tenuous. The Ervin committee was given no evidence that anyone told Nixon of the plans.

Destruction of Records

Undisputed facts. After the arrests at the Watergate on June 17, 1972, there was an orgy of paper shredding. Liddy quickly destroyed a sheaf of documents from his offices at the Nixon finance committee, presumably related to his political-espionage plans. Magruder similarly ordered his Watergate-related documents destroyed, including reports of intercepted conversations at Democratic headquarters. Strachan went through Haldeman's files and destroyed documents reporting the Liddy plan. Herbert Porter, the Nixon committee's scheduling director, shredded various expense receipts given him by Liddy. Later both Fred LaRue and

Herbert Kalmbach, Nixon's personal attorney, destroyed records on the amounts of money they had secretly distributed to the Watergate defendants or their attorneys. Acting FBI Director L. Patrick Gray burned documents taken from Hunt's safe. Nixon Finance Committee Chairman Maurice Stans, Treasurer Hugh Sloan Jr. and Kalmbach destroyed reports of campaign contributions received before a financing-disclosure law went into effect on April 7, 1972, although this destruction may not have had any direct connection with Watergate.

In dispute. Just who directed the destruction in each case is unclear. LaRue claimed that Mitchell suggested that Magruder have "a bonfire"; Mitchell denied that. Strachan claimed that Haldeman had suggested cleaning out his files; Haldeman had no such recollection. Porter said he shredded at Liddy's direction (Liddy has talked publicly to no one). Gray said he burned "politically sensitive" papers unrelated to Watergate at the suggestion of Ehrlichman and Dean; Ehrlichman said the papers were given to Gray for safekeeping and to guard against leaks.

Weight of evidence. The widespread burning and shredding, regardless of who ordered it, clearly indicates that an almost automatic cover-up of the origins of the Watergate operation began immediately after the break-in was discovered. Destruction of contribution records probably was intended mainly to protect the identity of donors. Yet the elimination of precise records on large amounts of campaign cash also hampered investigators trying to trace Liddy's operating funds.

What did Nixon know? There is no evidence that he knew anything about this matter. Many of the principals had ample reasons to protect themselves by destroying evidence without informing anyone else.

Misuse of the CIA and FBI

Undisputed facts. Shortly after the Watergate arrests, Nixon ordered Haldeman and Ehrlichman to meet with top officials of the CIA. They did so. Later that same day, newly installed Deputy CIA Director Vernon Walters told Gray that FBI attempts to trace money used by the wiretappers through Mexico might interfere with a covert CIA operation there. This slowed the FBI probe. Later Dean asked Walters whether the CIA might provide bail money and support the wiretappers if they were imprisoned. Both Walters and CIA Director Richard Helms decided that the White House was trying "to use" the agency. Walters, after checking further on what the agency was actually doing in Mexico, told Gray that there was no CIA operation in Mexico that could be compromised by the FBI. Gray concluded that there had been an attempt to interfere with the FBI investigation, and he warned the President on July 6, 1972, that "people on your staff are trying to mortally wound you." Nixon asked no questions, but told Gray to continue his investigation.

In dispute. Haldeman contended that he merely asked the CIA officials to find out whether the CIA had been involved in Watergate and whether they had some operation in Mexico that might be exposed. Both Helms and Walters claimed that Haldeman had introduced the subject as a potential political embarrassment, not a security matter. Walters said he was not asked to determine the facts, but was told by Haldeman to tell Gray to hold back the FBI's investigation in Mexico.

Weight of evidence. This is among the earliest and clearest instances of a White House effort to impede the investigation. The past CIA service of several of the arrested wiretappers made it seem logical at first that the CIA could provide a convenient cover for the Watergate operation, but Helms' instant denials to Haldeman of any CIA involvement promptly squelched any such notion.

What did Nixon know? Nixon said on May 22 that he had no intention of impeding any Watergate investigation, but was concerned about an FBI probe interfering with matters of national security. If his intent really was only to protect national security secrets, he failed to convey that to Haldeman or, through Ehrlichman, to Dean. As these aides relayed the President's instructions to Gray, Helms and Walters, the White House interest impressed those officials as highly political. The fact that Nixon asked no questions when Gray warned him about his aides' activities suggests that Nixon might well have known what those aides were trying to do.

Executive Clemency

Undisputed facts. Dean (through intermediaries John Caulfield and Anthony Ulasewicz) sent word to convicted wiretapper James McCord that he could expect executive clemency after perhaps a year in prison if he remained silent about any higher involvement in the burglary. McCord was told that the suggestion was coming "from the very highest levels of the White House." Even before the convicted wiretappers were sentenced, Ehrlichman and Dean asked Attorney General Richard Kleindienst at what point "executive pardons" could be granted to convicted criminals.

In dispute. Dean claimed that he transmitted the message to McCord after being told to do so by Mitchell, who had indicated that similar assurances of clemency had been given to Hunt, another convicted wiretapper. Mitchell flatly denied that he had given either Hunt or Dean such assurances. According to Dean, Ehrlichman, apparently after checking with Nixon, also told Colson that assurances of clemency could be given to Hunt. Ehrlichman heatedly denied this. Magruder testified that when he expressed concern about committing perjury about Liddy's assignments for the Nixon committee, Dean and Mitchell told him he could expect clemency, as well as family-support payments, if convicted. Mitchell denied making such a promise.

Weight of evidence. Whatever the precise level of authority it came from, word did get to some of the convicted burglars that they could expect to get out of prison after

serving relatively short terms if they kept quiet about who
had authorized the Watergate crimes.

What did Nixon know? Executive clemency can only be
offered by the President. If Nixon's aides were making such
offers, they risked directly implicating him. Dean contended
that Nixon told him on March 13 that he had discussed
clemency with both Ehrlichman and Colson. Nixon has
denied that, as have both Ehrlichman and Colson, and this
is one point on which the presidential tapes could prove
decisive.

Money for the Wiretappers

Undisputed facts. Some $420,000, taken mainly from
Nixon campaign contributions, was distributed covertly to
the seven Watergate defendants, their families and lawyers.
The deliverymen used telephone booths, storage lockers
and other public sites as drops so that the recipients would
never see them. One source of money was a $350,000 White
House cash fund that had been controlled by Haldeman.
Roughly half of the money was transmitted by Kalmbach,
the other half by LaRue. Dean helped arrange and direct
these payments.

In dispute. Dean claimed that Mitchell, Haldeman and
Ehrlichman all approved the payments. Kalmbach testified
that Ehrlichman specifically assured him that they were
proper, that Dean had authority to direct them and that
Kalmbach should continue to carry out Dean's instructions.
Both Ehrlichman and Mitchell denied these allegations.
Presidential aide Richard Moore relayed a request from either Haldeman or Ehrlichman (he was not sure which) that
Mitchell raise more money for the defendants. Moore said
that Mitchell refused. Dean testified that the money was intended to buy the silence of the defendants. Kalmbach and
Ehrlichman said it was meant for lawyers' fees or as a "hu-
manitarian" gesture. Haldeman admitted being aware of
the payments, but claimed he had not approved any, and
said he had made no judgments about their propriety.

Weight of evidence. If the White House was not seeking silence and was not trying to conceal the involvement of high officials, it would have been under no obligation to help defendants who had created such a politically embarrassing mess. The surreptitious delivery was strong evidence that all those involved knew it was wrong. The contrary claims seem to be belated efforts to avoid criminal prosecution.

What did Nixon know? Dean contended that he discussed these payoffs with Nixon, and that the President said it would be "no problem" to raise $1 million for this purpose. Haldeman, who listened to two tapes of this conversation, claimed that Nixon added a key phrase: "But it would be wrong." Only the tapes themselves can resolve this conflict.

The testimony does not legally prove that the President was an active participant in the cover-up (much less that he ordered or knew about the bugging). The damning testimony to that effect is the testimony of John Dean, which is still uncorroborated at key points. Dean's account has been challenged by Mitchell, Ehrlichman and Haldeman; their own credibility has been assailed in turn by other witnesses.

Although Nixon's involvement in the cover-up is not proved by courtroom standards, by any other rational standard it is extremely difficult to believe that he did not know of it or encourage it. He was warned early of cover-up activities undertaken by his closest aides; he then professed total unawareness for some nine months, despite his position at the apex of a tightly organized reporting system.

Throughout all the internal conflicts and ambiguities in the testimony, an overall pattern seems clear. Unwilling to trust regular agencies of Government to deal with genuine, though exaggerated, threats to domestic order, Nixon approved illegal means to fight them. When those were rejected by self-protecting bureaucrats, he created his own White House squad of undercover operators. They used some of these same illegal tactics against whatever forces the White House considered threatening, whether a Daniel Ellsberg, a Dita Beard or a talkative official. Eventually they were used against the Democrats.

Aside from these specific acts, the Watergate hearings produced evidence of an alarming atmosphere around the President. Whether it was John Ehrlichman's defense of spying on the drinking and sexual habits of politicians, John Dean's advocacy of using agencies of Government to "screw our political enemies," or Bob Haldeman's desire to "put out the story" of Communist money falsely alleged to be supporting Democratic candidates, an amorality prevailed that went well beyond normal standards of politics. It degraded the White House.

There was too the incessant secret taping, most notably by Nixon himself. The untested technicality of executive privilege to protect the President's tapes, whatever its constitutional merits, seems insufficient cause to withhold evidence that might dispose of some of the accusations against him. Until and unless further evidence or explanations emerge from the President's expected statement, that is where the matter stands.

THE MAN IN THE JUDICIARY [4]

There was little ennobling in the broad shape of human affairs in 1973. Mankind progressed haltingly, if at all, in its tortuous quest for greater wisdom in the conduct of international relations and greater brotherhood among individuals. The United States continued to improve relations with China and clung to a strained détente with the Soviet Union. But political sentiments elsewhere still were expressed in the blood language of terrorist bombs and bullets, from Belfast to Madrid, Rome to Khartoum. Once more men died in battles on the hot sands of the Sinai and in the barren Golan Heights. The first freely elected Marx-

[4] From "Judge John Sirica: Standing Firm for the Primacy of Law." *Time*. 1:8+. Ja. 7, '74. Reprinted by permission from *Time*, the weekly newsmagazine; copyright Time Inc.

ist leader in the world was killed in a right-wing rebellion in Chile; a changing of the guardians refurbished authoritarian rule in Greece. For Americans, the dying finally ended in the paddyfields and jungles of Vietnam, but more than fifty thousand Vietnamese killed each other after the long-awaited "peace."

Yet more than any other event, it was the multifaceted Watergate affair, the worst political scandal in US history, that dominated the news in 1973. As it gradually unfolded, involving more and more areas of President Richard Nixon's Administration, it revealed a shocking disdain for both the spirit and the letter of the law at the highest levels of Government. Ultimately, not only the primacy of the rule of law on which the American system rests but the presidency of Nixon stood challenged, plunging the United States into a grave governmental crisis. Fittingly, it was the American legal system, which had trained so many of the malefactors caught in the Watergate web, that came to the rescue.

One judge, stubbornly and doggedly pursuing the truth in his courtroom regardless of its political implications, forced Watergate into the light of investigative day. One judge, insisting that not all the panoply of the presidency entitled Nixon to withhold material evidence from the Watergate prosecutors, brought the White House tapes and documents out of hiding. For these deeds, and as a symbol of the American judiciary's insistence on the priority of law throughout the sordid Watergate saga of 1973, *Time*'s Man of the Year is Federal Judge John Joseph Sirica.

A Judicial Search for Truth and Justice

Set against the widespread abuse of executive power exemplified by Watergate, Sirica's performance was particularly reassuring as a testimony to the integrity of the institution he represents. Of proudly humble origins and with no pretensions to legal erudition, Sirica, at sixty-nine, culminated his career only a year from retirement as chief judge of the United States District Court for Washington, D.C. He had from the outset no ambition other than to do his job in the Watergate cases: find the truth, see that justice was done.

Modest and unimposing in speech and stature out of court, the five-feet-six-inch jurist towered and glowered from his bench, openly indignant at what he considered evasions and deceptions in testimony before him. He simply did not believe that the seven lowly burglars who had wiretapped Democratic National Committe headquarters at Washington's Watergate complex in June 1972 were a self-starting team working alone. Injudicially, some have argued, but undeniably in the higher national interest, as others would insist, he applied pressure until he got a scandal-bursting response. Once James W. McCord Jr. began to talk, the White House conspiracy to keep Watergate "a third-rate burglary" came apart at the seams.

Sirica used his same rugged courtroom common sense to cope with the challenge of a historic constitutional clash between branches of Government. Even a President must respond to subpoenas for evidence in criminal cases, Sirica ruled. Judges, not the President, must ultimately decide whether claims of executive privilege to withhold such evidence are valid. Presidents, in short, are not above the law. The Circuit Court of Appeals for the District of Columbia upheld him; and in the end, Nixon gave up, partly because he feared that the Supreme Court would also see it Sirica's way.

Other characters in the Watergate drama, most notably the President around whom the whole affair revolved, played major roles. Yet Nixon, to his own detriment, never took charge of the scandal, continually reacting to events rather than shaping them. The remarkable Senator Sam Ervin, who rose spectacularly as a national folk hero in chairing the historic Senate Watergate hearings, employed literary allusions and unabashed outrage to effectively belittle the many evasive and immoral Nixon men who came before him.

Archibald
fused to accept
to circumvent
tapes, and public
sist from seeking
Nixon, Cox bowed
a fire storm of pr
General Elliot Rich
of integrity in the
by defying the White
ardson resigned instead,
tion.

grave doubts about Nixon's
blanket denials, lavish cla
vocations of national
fications, previous
multiple The
sisted. The
sudden
Cand
we

The Allegations Ag

But as the scandal ballooned ...tical
burglary and its cover-up, wide-ran, ...ions against
Nixon himself became part of the se.uid affair. They included contentions that Nixon had: (1) intervened in an
antitrust action against ITT in return for political contributions; (2) raised milk support prices and reduced dairy
imports for similar considerations; (3) issued orders leading
to the burglary of the office of Daniel Ellsberg's psychiatrist;
(4) offered to appoint the judge in the Ellsberg case FBI
director, as a means of influencing his decision in the case;
(5) ordered or condoned illegal wiretapping and other
"White House horrors" perpetrated by his self-appointed
"plumbers"; (6) obstructed justice by firing Prosecutor Cox;
(7) directed or knew about the solicitation of illegal campaign contributions from corporations; (8) misused public
funds in improving his residences in Key Biscayne and San
Clemente; (9) failed to pay his proper share of Federal and
California income taxes; (10) had altered or disposed of
some presidential Watergate tapes.

Richard Nixon's culpability is not yet clear, although
the president of almost anything else would have been
quickly forced to resign by a scandal infecting so much of
his organization. Moreover, the strange oscillations in White
House attitudes toward the various investigations raised

innocence. First there were
ms of executive privilege and in-
security. Then came repeated clari-
statements declared "inoperative," and
es of full disclosure. Subpoenas were re-
ersistent Special Prosecutor was fired. Next a
elding to the courts, followed by an Operation
r that was far from candid, claims that crucial tapes
e "nonexistent" and the revelation of a mysterious flaw
in one recording. Observes *Time* Washington Bureau Chief
Hugh Sidey: "It all falls into place, it all makes sense, if
one makes a very simple assumption: Nixon is guilty—he
knew what his men were doing and, indeed, directed them."
Otherwise, it was all irrational behavior—and that, too,
would be frightening in a President. As a result, Nixon,
who began the year as the most decisively reelected President in US history, ended it facing demands for his resignation and an impeachment inquiry by the Judiciary committee of the House of Representatives.

As 1973 began, the Watergate wiretapping was widely
regarded as a mysterious political operation, its origins un-
known and its seriousness unappreciated. Candidate George
McGovern had been unable to stir much interest in it as a
campaign issue. Except for dogged digging by a small seg-
ment of the US press, most notably the Washington *Post*
and *Time*, the entire matter might have faded from public
view.

While the news stories traced some links between the
White House and the electronic eavesdropping on the
Democrats, the Justice department prepared to handle the
case routinely. Henry Petersen, head of the department's
criminal division, assigned a team of bright but junior
prosecutors, including Earl J. Silbert, Seymour Glanzer and
Donald Campbell, to the task. At Petersen's direction, they
showed little zeal for tracing the source of the funds used by
the men arrested at the Watergate or determining who had
authorized the politically motivated crime.

The case of the seven original defendants did not look all that ordinary to Judge Sirica, who had been reading the newspapers and later told some reporters: "I was only asking myself the same questions you were." As chief judge of the District Court, he had the duty to assign the case to one of fifteen judges—and he took it himself. That was partly because he had a relatively light docket at the time, but also because he felt that if he as a Republican judge handled the matter, and did so fairly and aggressively, no charges could be leveled that partisanship had entered the judicial process.

The Appearance of Justice Must Prevail

Thus on January 11, ten days before Nixon was inaugurated for his second term in a mood of festive partying and high spirits, Sirica presided solemnly in his fifth-floor courtroom in the beige United States Court House and served notice that he regarded the Watergate burglary as a far from simple matter. E. Howard Hunt Jr., sometime White House consultant, CIA agent and mystery novelist, offered to plead guilty to three of the six charges against him as one of the seven men arrested for the Watergate wiretapping-burglary. In this case, answered Sirica, the public would have to be assured that not only "the substance of justice" but also "the appearance of justice" was preserved. Also, because "of the apparent strength of the Government's case" against him, Hunt would have to plead guilty to all six counts or go to trial for each. Hunt admitted his guilt on all of them.

"Don't pull any punches—you give me straight answers," warned Sirica when the four Cuban Americans arrested at the Watergate pleaded guilty four days later. If anyone else was involved, Sirica added, "I want to know it and the grand jury wants to know it." The four insisted that the conspiracy stopped at the low levels of their arrested leaders: Hunt; G. Gordon Liddy, another former White House consultant and counsel for Nixon's 1972 reelection finance committee; and James W. McCord Jr., a former CIA electronic-eavesdropping expert and security chief for Nixon's reelection committee. Where did they get the money to carry out their operation? They did not know. Snapped Sirica: "Well, I'm sorry, but I don't believe you."

Sirica was still skeptical when the Government's main witness, former FBI Agent Alfred C. Baldwin, admitted at the trial of Liddy and McCord that he had monitored many of the conversations of Democrats on a radio receiver in the Howard Johnson's motel across the street from the Watergate. But Baldwin also insisted that he could not recall to whom at the Nixon reelection committee he had delivered records of the intercepted talks. "Here you are an FBI agent and you want the court and jury to belive that you gave [them] to some guard you hardly knew? Is that your testimony?" asked Sirica. It was indeed.

With the jury out of the courtroom, Sirica dismissed as "ridiculous, frankly" the claim by McCord's attorney, Gerald Alch, that McCord had helped bug the Democrats in hopes of detecting plans of radicals for acts of violence against Republicans during the campaign. If McCord really believed that, Sirica suggested, he should have called police, the FBI or the Secret Service. Well, could McCord's defense be based on the claim that he had no criminal intent? "You may argue it," Sirica told Alch. "Whether the jury will belive you is another story."

The jury did not, finding both McCord and Liddy guilty on January 30 of burglary, wiretapping and attempted bugging. At a bail hearing for the two conspirators, Sirica urged the Government's prosecutors to put certain Nixon officials "under oath in the grand jury room." At least one, former Commerce Secretary Maurice Stans, had been permitted by the prosecution to submit a sworn statement to the grand jury in lieu of testifying. "I am still not satisfied that all of the pertinent facts have been produced before an American jury," Sirica declared. He reminded the prosecutors of a list of persons he wanted them to question again.

Following judicial routine, Sirica ordered presentencing

investigations for all seven defendants. But going beyond normal procedure, he let the convicted men know that the severity of sentences would depend heavily on the degree to which they cooperated with probation officers and investigators still probing the Watergate crimes. One potential truth-baring forum looming ahead at the time was that of Sam Ervin's Senate Select Committee. Sirica welcomed the hearings despite the fact that they could complicate some criminal prosecutions. "Not only as a judge but as one of millions of Americans who are looking for certain answers," Sirica said, he hoped the Ervin committee could "get to the bottom of what happened in this case."

The combination of the impending hearings, twinges of conscience, and Sirica's not very veiled hints at severe sentences was too much for one of the previously uncommunicative conspirators. On March 20 Sirica stepped out of his chambers and into his office reception area to find James McCord standing there with a letter in his hand. A clerk told the startled judge that McCord wanted to see him privately. Sirica, who never allows a defendant or convicted individual to approach him privately before sentencing, quickly retreated to his chambers and ordered McCord to leave. He said McCord would have to hand any communication to his probation officer on a lower floor.

For Sirica, it was an awkward situation. Perhaps McCord was offering incriminating information on others. But what if the envelope contained money, and some sinister plot to frame the judge was under way? Should he have any private dealings at all with McCord, if only to accept a letter? Should he just turn the envelope over to Government prosecutors and let them open it? But what if it contained something McCord did not want even the prosecutors to know?

Sirica resolved the matter instinctively, reverting to a career-long tendency to get everything possible on the official record. He summoned his two law clerks, a court reporter, a bailiff, and the probation officer with the letter.

Sirica would open it only in their presence and he would read it immediately into the record. As he did so, the implications of McCord's message immediately hit Sirica. "I knew this might throw light on things we suspected but didn't know," he explained later. "It convinced me I'd done exactly the right thing in asking all those questions."

Three days later, Sirica acted on another of his habits: when in doubt, make matters public. He read the McCord letter to a crowded courtroom. McCord had written that he feared "retaliatory measures against me, my family and my friends," said he did not trust the regular investigatory agencies enough to give them the information but felt he must disclose that: (1) political pressures from high officials had been "applied to the defendants to plead guilty and remain silent"; (2) perjury masking the motivations of the defendants had occurred during the McCord-Liddy trial; and (3) "others involved in the Watergate operation were not identified during the trial, when they could have been by those testifying." After he had read the letter and watched newsmen rush for telephones, the import struck Sirica again, almost like a physical blow. He felt pains in his chest, ordered a recess in the proceedings and retired to his chambers to rest.

When McCord later detailed his charges to Government and Senate investigators, he claimed he had been told that former Attorney General John Mitchell had approved the Watergate wiretapping plans, that all the defendants had been given regular installments of payoff money to keep quiet, that he and others had been promised executive clemency in return for their silence after serving short prison terms, and that this offer came from the White House. McCord's sources of information were Liddy and Hunt, making his own testimony hearsay and thus legally inconclusive in a criminal case. But the fact that McCord was talking broke the conspiracy of silence—and blew open the whole scandal.

Sirica then deferred sentencing McCord. But in the most

controversial act in his entire handling of the Watergate affair, he also kept the pressure on the other convicted conspirators to talk too by giving them harsh provisional sentences ranging up to forty years. He called their crimes "sordid, despicable and thoroughly reprehensible." He promised to review the sentences later and said that the final sentencing "would depend on your full cooperation with the grand jury and the Senate Select Committee." Sirica's expressed purpose: "Some good can and should come from a revelation of sinister conduct whenever and wherever such conduct exists."

Solid evidence that the extreme sentences would not be finally imposed came when Sirica sentenced Liddy, the one conspirator who apparently intended to live up to the *omertà* training of a clandestine agent by stubbornly remaining silent. Liddy was given a term of from six years and eight months to twenty years. When he was granted immunity against further prosecution and recalled before the grand jury for questioning about other conspirators, he still balked—so Sirica on April 3 gave him an additional prison term for contempt of court. Frankly conceding that he was wielding a judicial club, Sirica said that the aim was "to give meaning and coercive impact to the court's contempt powers."

At a higher level, the cover-up was now crumbling. White House Counsel John Dean had warned Nixon on March 21 that "there was a cancer growing on the presidency." Dean spirited documents from his own files out of the White House, put them in a bank safe-deposit box and gave the keys to Sirica. When the White House on May 14 asked Sirica to return the Dean documents, the judge refused. He would keep the originals and give copies to new Watergate Special Prosecutor Archibald Cox and the Ervin committee staff.

Sirica complied with a Senate committee request by giving limited immunity against prosecution to Dean and another suddenly talkative witness, Jeb Stuart Magruder, deputy director of Nixon's reelection committee. They could still be prosecuted, but not on the basis of evidence gleaned solely from their televised testimony. Sirica also flashed a judicial green light for the hearings to proceed as planned by rejecting a Cox motion that television and radio coverage of Dean's and Magruder's testimony be banned. Cox had argued that the wide publicity could jeopardize future criminal cases against individuals.

The Parade Before the Ervin Committee

Throughout much of the summer, the nation's attention shifted from courtroom to caucus room as the familiar Watergate names turned into unforgettable images on America's television screens. This was television's greatest contribution yet to public understanding of a historic and confusing event—and the Watergate intrigue in all its ramifications was surely one of the most complex and convoluted stories in American political history. More than all of the news accounts, more than the proceedings in Judge Sirica's courtroom, the Senate Watergate hearings dramatized the issues and personalities, permitting millions of Americans to make up their own minds about whom to believe and whom to doubt.

Some of the once faceless Nixon operatives ruefully admitted their own guilty roles in the several Watergate conspiracies. Others unconvincingly denied any participation by themselves or anyone at the White House. But only the relatively powerless John Dean, tainted but nevertheless courageous in his turncoat testimony, made grave accusations of the President's participation in the cover-up. His chilling tale, conveyed in a lifeless baritone, was sharply denied by such far more influential and shrewd Nixon intimates as H. R. Haldeman, John Ehrlichman and John Mitchell.

Nixon stood on his earlier claims that he had known nothing of the wiretapping in advance, never approved clemency for the defendants, was unaware of payoffs to them and played no part in the conspiracy to conceal. Then, dramatically, a means to break the testimonial impasse was revealed: Alexander Butterfield, a former White House aide (now head of the FAA [Federal Aviation Administration]), told the Ervin committee that most of the President's White House meetings and telephone calls had been secretly recorded. The Senate committee and Prosecutor Cox promptly issued subpoenas for key tapes.

That brought Judge Sirica back on center stage and in an unfamiliar and challenging role. In sixteen years on the Federal bench, Sirica had handled a wide gamut of criminal trials and civil suits, including highly complex antitrust cases. But now he was being asked to rule on an unprecedented claim by the executive branch that a President is immune from subpoenas because the courts have no power to enforce any order against him; that only the impeachment process of Congress can touch him. Moreover, argued Nixon's legal consultant, University of Texas Law Professor Charles Alan Wright, Nixon's tapes were protected by the unwritten doctrine of executive privilege. Only the President had the power to decide which of his documents were so privileged or which might also endanger national security if made public. At issue, contended Wright, was "nothing less than the continued existence of the presidency as a functioning institution."

Sirica did not agree. In an opinion praised by some legal scholars as unexpectedly erudite, he wrote that he was "extremely reluctant to finally stand against a declaration of the President of the United States on any but the strongest possible evidence." Nonetheless, he would have to examine the tapes himself in order to determine whether the President's case for not yielding them was valid. "In all candor," Sirica said, "the court fails to perceive any reason for suspending the power of courts to get evidence and rule on questions of privilege in criminal matters simply because it is the President of the United States who holds the evidence." Asked Sirica rhetorically: "What distinctive quality of the presidency permits its incumbent to withhold evidence? To argue that the need for presidential privacy justifies it is not persuasive." As for impeachment, that could be "the final remedy" in "the most excessive cases," but "the courts have always enjoyed the good faith of the executive branch." Sirica, in short, would not expect Nixon to ignore a court order.

White House Turnabout on Giving Up Tapes

Sirica had the satisfaction of seeing his opinion essentially upheld by the Circuit Court of Appeals, which observed: "Though the President is elected by nationwide ballot and is often said to represent all the people, he does not embody the nation's sovereignty. He is not above the law's commands."

On October 19 Nixon announced that he would not appeal the case to the Supreme Court. Instead, he would make available a summary of each of the subpoenaed tapes and would allow Senator John Stennis of Mississippi to listen to the tapes to see if the summary was accurate. There was no reason for Prosecutor Cox to accept that unilateral arrangement, since he had a far better chance of getting the tapes themselves under Sirica's order. So Cox objected—and was fired by Nixon. Declared Cox after he was ousted: "Whether ours shall continue to be a government of laws and not of men is now for Congress and ultimately the American people to decide."

The clamor of public protest that followed the Cox dismissal and the virtually simultaneous resignations of Attorney General Elliot Richardson and Deputy Attorney General William Ruckelshaus shocked the White House. At first Counselor Wright, on the following Tuesday, October 23, was prepared to argue before Sirica that the Stennis compromise met the thrust of the Court of Appeals' suggestion that an out-of-court solution to the tapes impasse be found. But clearly it did not meet Sirica's order to produce the tapes. Although Sirica will not say what he intended to do about it, he does admit that he "was prepared to act." Other judicial sources expected him eventually to cite the President for contempt of court. Suddenly, however, Nixon changed his mind, ordered Wright to tell Sirica that he would "fully comply" with the subpoenas for the tapes. When Wright did so, astonishing almost everyone in Sirica's courtroom, the clearly incredulous judge smiled broadly and said: "Mr. Wright, the court is very happy the President has reached this decision."

The court was not at all happy, however, when another White House counsel, J. Fred Buzhardt, informed Sirica on October 30 that two of the nine subpoenaed tapes were "nonexistent" because they had never been made. Sirica scowled even more sternly on November 21 when Buzhardt sheepishly revealed another problem with the tapes: eighteen minutes of a Nixon conversation with Chief of Staff Haldeman—the only part of the recording about Watergate—had been obliterated by a mysterious overriding hum. Again, Sirica ordered public hearings on this curious dwindling of the tapes evidence.

Those unusual fact-finding proceedings produced the bizarre testimony of Rose Mary Woods, Nixon's longtime personal secretary. She said she had inadvertently kept her left foot on the pedal of a tape recorder while stretching awkwardly behind her to answer a telephone call, at the same time mistakenly pushing the "record" button on the machine—and thereby erasing perhaps five minutes (but not eighteen) of the taped conversation. Asked in Perry Mason–style by Jill Wine Volner, an assistant special prosecutor, to reenact this, Miss Woods reached for the imaginary phone—and lifted her left foot. Sirica ordered all the tapes to be examined by a panel of technical experts for "any evidence of tampering."

While the technicians continued their studies—an undertaking Sirica described as potentially "most important and conclusive"—he and his young law clerk, Todd Christofferson, listened to the tapes through headphones in a jury room. Sirica upheld claims of executive privilege or irrelevance on all or parts of three tapes, turning five over to the new special prosecutor, Leon Jaworski, and the grand jury. Although constricted, the tapes still were expected to be helpful in determining who had been more truthful, Nixon or Dean.

Convinced that legal processes were well in motion to get at Watergate truths, Sirica sentenced the long-jailed burglars to relatively light terms; the minimums ranged from one year to thirty months, much of the time already served. Said Sirica: "I've given you the lowest minimum I thought justified."

The Argument Over Sirica's Tactics and Conduct

Despite that outcome, Sirica has been severely criticized by some legal authorities for using the provisional-sentencing procedure as a device to get the defendants to cooperate with investigators. "We must be concerned about a Federal judge —no matter how worthy his motives or how much we may applaud his results—using the criminal-sentencing process as a means and tool for further criminal investigation of others," contends Chesterfield Smith, president of the American Bar Association. The association's president-elect, James Fellers of Oklahoma City, much admires Sirica and his Watergate role but likens the sentencing tactic to "the torture rack and the Spanish Inquisition." Argues Law Dean Monroe Freedman of Hofstra University: "Sirica deserves to be censured for becoming the prosecutor himself." The University of Chicago's Law Professor Philip Kurland considers the harsh original sentences "a form of extortion."

Sirica defends his action on grounds that no one seriously expected those severe sentences to be made final and that the law makes it mandatory that any provisional sentence must be the maximum possible; he did not have discretion to make it lower. Moreover, it could be argued that Sirica's efforts to determine the true motives and origins of the crime were relevant to his decision on how severely finally to punish the defendants. Yet it is also true that the men had every legal right to remain silent and that this particular use of provisional sentencing, while technically lawful, could infringe on their civil rights. Sirica, not much given to mulling over law theory, is unrepentant. To critics of his actions, including his persistent questioning of defendants from the bench, he has replied: "I'm glad I did it. If I had it to do over, I would do the same—and that's the end of that."

Many of Sirica's colleagues on benches around the country seem to agree with him. More broadly, his handling of the Watergate cases is widely seen as a vindication of the legal system at a time of great stress. Chief Judge David Bazelon, who heads the United States Circuit Court of Appeals for the District of Columbia, which has sometimes reversed Sirica rulings, contends that "Sirica became enraged not because he believed he was being lied to personally, but because he thought the court was being lied to. He has humility, which is not a universal virtue among judges." Former ABA [American Bar Association] President Bernard Segal calls Sirica "a shining light. He's shown firmness, understanding and great integrity." Declares a former partner of Sirica's in the Washington law firm of Hogan & Hartson: "He was the worst judge the Administration could have had on this case. He's a deep-dyed Republican who is genuinely outraged at what's happening in the party that put him on the bench."

Exposure of wrongdoing is, of course, the first requisite in achieving justice—and Sirica deserves the prime credit for taking those vital initial steps. Whether justice and law in the end will prevail still depends on the investigation by Prosecutor Jaworski and his determined staff, the outcome of numerous individual trials, and what may still be learned —and done about—the President's actions in the many Watergate-related improprieties. Sirica will continue to play a role in that process since he intends to remain an active judge on the bench even after he retires as chief judge in March. . . .

The future criminal cases, however, may not answer a key question: How could so much have suddenly gone so wrong? Certainly a longtime trend toward an increasingly dominant US presidency was a factor. In a development beginning with Franklin Roosevelt, vastly enhanced by the romantic Camelot atmosphere surrounding John Kennedy, too much authority has been given by Americans to their Presidents and too much has been expected of them. Harvard Divinity Professor Harvey Cox goes so far as to contend that the US public surrounds the Oval Office with a mystique that approaches "a national quasi-religious cultism."

Yet there is something unique in the Nixon character and the men he chose to aid him that spawned Watergate. Despite his intention of "returning power to the people," Nixon drew authority about him like a blanket of insulation—and waved it over domineering aides responsible only to himself. Unchecked by the accountability of Cabinet officers, who must look to the traditions of their office, answer to congressional committees and worry about legalities and public opinion, these *apparatchik* White House guardians cherished secrecy and told Nixon only what he wanted to hear.

The President in turn seemed at ease solely with such automatic yes men and relatively anonymous associates, but apparently confided fully not even in them. Yet he shared powerful prejudices with them, most dangerously a siege mentality in which so many other vague classifications of Americans—liberals, antiwar radicals, academic intellectuals, Eastern sophisticates, the press—were seen as enemies, akin to unfriendly foreign powers. They were to be subverted, subjected to surveillance and eavesdropping, and "screwed" by agencies of Government. Nixon's reelection campaign became a crusade in which any means were seen as justified to keep all those fearful foes out of power. National security was equated with Nixon security.

But how could so many attorneys, trained in concepts of justice and the rule of law, become involved? Orville H. Schell Jr., president of the New York City Bar Association, blames this on a tendency of many lawyers today to forgo their critical independence and to serve as in-house counsels for corporations, foundations and Government. Their powerful clients thus become their bosses; the lawyer's aim is to please, not to advise that what the boss wants done may be wrong. One law school dean is less charitable in faulting such a broad trend. He blames Nixon for hiring "legal midgets—underclass lawyers. That's why he was so surprised by the really classy guys like Cox, Richardson and Ruckelshaus."

Yet it is the legal profession that has, however belatedly and at first by a narrow edge, finally become most aroused about the transgressions against law and the Constitution that make up the dismal scandal. While the profession has moved forcefully through such men as Sirica, Cox and Richardson to acquit itself, it is still on trial, and whether justice will finally prevail is still in doubt.

No Single Outcome Can Please Everyone

"We don't have a victory of good; we just have an exposure of evil," observes Professor Kurland. "Nothing has been triumphant but cynicism." Stanford Law Professor Anthony Amsterdam worries whether justice can possibly be done when the criminal evidence has been held up for so long by those who might be guilty. "It is as if in a bank robbery all evidence were given to the robber to hold for two years before trial."

Certainly, if justice is not seen as prevailing by most Americans in the many trials still to emerge from the affair, a deepening cynicism and a rootless everybody-does-it syndrome of irresponsibility for individual acts may be Watergate's more lasting legacy. Whatever the outcome—most crucially including the fairness and thoroughness with which the President's political fate is resolved—millions of Americans will still consider the result wrong. Watergate thus is bound to leave a lingering bitterness among at least a minority of Americans.

Yet the nation may well be poised on a fateful fulcrum that will either tip predominant sentiment toward a new faith in its fundamental institutions—including Congress, the Constitution and the courts—or send it into a trough of public despair and anomie. The direction will depend to a large degree upon how many members of Congress, Government prosecutors, judges, jurors—and, indeed, the vast public jury—try to emulate the nonpartisan determination and faith of Judge John Sirica, who insists with simple sincerity that "if the truth just comes out, we'll all be all right."

III. THE GROWTH OF PRESIDENTIAL POWER

EDITOR'S INTRODUCTION

Watergate is enough of an issue to have raised questions about the presidency. But the vigor with which Congress seized on the issue betrayed that it had deeper grievances than Watergate.

The Constitution provides that the three branches of government—executive, legislative, and judicial—be roughly equal in power. The whole system of checks and balances presupposes equal partners. But to the resentment of Congress the Executive has been increasingly growing stronger. Perhaps the most notable escalation of White House power came in the 1930s under the Administration of Franklin D. Roosevelt. Later, in the crisis atmosphere of the Cold War, each White House occupant seemed to graft even more power onto the existing base. Indeed, in recent years, the presidency of the United States has become known as the most powerful elective office on earth.

Articles in this section detail this growing power and the imbalance between Congress and the presidency. The first excerpt states the obvious—that beyond the immediate issue of Watergate lie congressional concerns about the President's decreasing measure of accountability. The second article, from a speech by a political scientist, details how the presidency has grown to its present command of power. The third, a statement of opinion, notes that the Executive has now probably become more powerful than the Constitution intended it to be.

The last articles in this section, however, point out a paradox. Modern circumstances and conditions are such that they result in additional presidential power even without the President's asking for it. The fourth article, for instance, shows that the press builds the President's popular support with the public by the constant coverage it gives him. The fifth selection notes that the White House was tightening its grip on the ever mounting number of Government jobs available. And the final piece in the section touches on a real irony. Much as Congress resents the growth of the executive branch, it contributes directly to the increase. When the energy crisis gripped the nation in the fall and winter of 1973, Congress hastily gave President Nixon wide emergency powers to deal with the dilemma. It gave him these powers at the same time that the hue and cry for impeachment was beginning to be transformed into congressional action.

BEYOND WATERGATE [1]

At the heart of the current contest between the President and Congress is the question of accountability—specifically the accountability of those who govern to those who are governed in a democratic society. Critics of Richard M. Nixon contend that he is assuming powers that rightfully belong to the legislative branch of government, the branch most open to public scrutiny in its day-to-day deliberations and hence most accountable to the voter in its actions.

The decisions of Congress are reached by a protracted process involving public hearings and debates that keep the channels of popular pressure open for many weeks and months while proposed legislation is being considered. Final determination of policy is usually the product of a consensus after all shades of opinion have been heard. This process contrasts with the solitary decision making of a President, who is only rarely under any constitutional obligation to consult with anyone or even to give out advance signals before taking actions of momentous import to the nation.

[1] From "Presidential Accountability," report by Helen B. Shaffer, staff writer. *Editorial Research Reports.* v 1, no 9:167-8. Mr. 7, '73. Reprinted by permission.

Presidents are accountable in the sense that they usually cannot succeed for long in the exercise of power unless they can count on the support of a wide majority of the citizenry. Normally, the instrument of popular restraint on an over-reaching President is Congress, whose members tend to be jealous of legislative prerogatives. But a daring or determined President may be undaunted by outcries from Congress. He may acquire massive support by appealing to the nation over the head of Congress on an issue. Or he may build up so much trust in his leadership that he can rely on public acceptance of his actions, however arbitrary and even discomfiting, and thus overcome any resistance that might be manifested in Congress.

It is precisely this power of the President to act at some distance from direct accountability to the people which has given concern whenever a confrontation between the White House and Congress shapes up, as it is shaping up now. The awe with which Americans regard the presidential office has always given the Chief Executive an advantage when he speaks from the White House—a "bully pulpit," as Theodore Roosevelt described it. This advantage has greatly expanded in modern times. The President can now speak to the entire nation, at a time of his own choosing, without the impediment of heckling or rebuttal, and with the immense resources of image-making techniques at his disposal. By limiting the number of press conferences and exercising firm command over the manner in which they are conducted, he can greatly reduce the potentiality of this institution for making a President answerable to his critics.

The distance between the President and direct accountability to the people has been further stretched by the increasing complexity of public issues and the enormous scope of governmental functions. With the validity of decisions on public policy depending more and more on specialist expertise, the average citizen is inclined to let the man at the top make those decisions without objection. It is this combination of developments that has given rise to fear that a

modern President, while seeming to adhere to the principle
of accountability by addressing himself at carefully chosen
intervals to the people, may succeed in obtaining near-
dictatorial power.

WHY THE PRESIDENCY GROWS STRONGER [2]

The presidency puts too much power in one man. That
proposition is heard increasingly these days, for a decade
of war in Vietnam and now the Watergate affair have revealed a vast potential for abuse of the enormous power that
is entrusted to a single human being. And the realization has
come as something of a shock. After all, this was exactly
what the Founding Fathers, reacting against the tyranny of
George III, were supposedly striving to prevent. We were
brought up to believe that the unique American contribution to the art of government was "checks and balances."

We were lulled into complacency because we thought the
system of checks and balances was more pervasive than it is.
The deadlocks we have so often witnessed occur in a particular process of government—the legislative process—and
what applies to the legislative power does not necessarily
apply to the executive power. Legislation is a shared responsibility; both the President and the Congress have a
veto. But once a law is enacted, the power to carry it out is
not shared between President and Congress, for the Constitution vests the executive power in the President alone.

The assignment of executive power to the President does
not mean that the other branches of government do not
exercise some checks. They do get involved in the execution
of the laws, in half a dozen ways. But these checks, taken
altogether, have always been severely limited in their practical effect.

[2] Article entitled "Needed: A Workable Check on the Presidency," by James
L. Sundquist. *Brookings Bulletin*. 10:7-11. Fall '73. © 1973 by the Brookings
Institution, Washington, D.C. Mr. Sundquist is a senior fellow in Brookings'
Governmental Studies program. The article stems from his remarks at a confer-
ence on the lessons of Watergate, held at the Washington (D.C.) Journalism
Center in October 1973.

The courts can check the President and often have, as when [on June 2, 1952] they ordered Harry Truman to return the seized steel plants to their owners. But this power is limited to cases of actual lawbreaking; the judicial process imposes no check on presidential actions that are merely unwise or improper. Moreover, in the broad area of national security and foreign affairs, it is difficult to find cases that can be taken into court.

Impeachment can be seen as an extreme form of judicial process; as such, it has at least as many limitations as court proceedings. "High crimes and misdemeanors" must be proved. In today's meanings of those words (which are the meanings the Congress acts on, though a case can be made that the phrase carried a looser meaning when it was written into the Constitution), a President who has simply lost his capacity to lead and govern because of bungling, betrayal by ill-chosen subordinates, or any of the other weaknesses that can lead to misuse of presidential power, cannot for that reason be relieved of power.

The Senate's power to confirm appointments is not an effective check, for the obvious reasons that the Senate cannot know in advance which presidential appointees are going to abuse their power. When the names of John Mitchell and Maurice Stans were presented for confirmation, no one could have foreseen that they would be indicted four years later. If the Senate could *unconfirm* appointments, that would be a real check, but such power—for good reason— was not granted by the Constitution.

If the President does something the majority in Congress disapproves, it can amend the law to prevent the President from doing it again. But this possibility is more theory than fact. The President retains the power of veto, and if he wants to go on doing what the congressional majority objects to, a minority of one third plus one of either house is sufficient to sustain his veto. Nor can an amendment usually be made retroactive to force a reversal of what the President has already done. Moreover, to curtail the executive power by law is liable to prevent the President from accomplishing ends that in the congressional views are still desirable.

Nor is the power of the purse an effective check. Since appropriation bills are only a form of legislation, attempts to control the President through the budget encounter the same difficulties as in attempting to control him through amending substantive law. He can veto bills carrying unpalatable riders, and his vetoes will usually be sustained. To cut funds is no corrective for maladministration.

Lastly, in order to legislate and appropriate, the Congress through its committees may obtain information on how the laws are carried out, using subpoenas if necessary. Through this process, senators and congressmen can kibitz, entreat, heckle, and threaten, and these methods are often effective. But they cannot compel a determined President to change his course.

A common weakness of almost all these checks and balances is that they operate after the fact, often long after. The Congress has been able to exercise a review power in the case of both Vietnam and Watergate—and in the Watergate affair judicial checks have been operating too—but only long after the damage has been done. The one exception, Senate confirmation, operates only before the fact, sometimes long before. None of the checks and balances operate during or close to the fact, which is when the abuse of power needs to be prevented.

The Expanding Government

These checks and balances, weak as they have been throughout our history, have been further weakened by several trends that for the most part are not reversible. While the Federal Government's budget has increased by 500 percent in a quarter century and the Government has been thrust into a multiplicity of new activities, the capacity of the Congress to check executive operations has not increased on anything like the same scale. Nor can the Congress be expected to keep pace, no matter how much it improves itself through reorganizing, strengthening its staff, electing stronger leaders, or attending to its duties with greater diligence. No matter how it changes its practices, its checks and balances will still have to be exercised through difficult, demanding work by individual members, acting mainly in committees. As the size and scope of Government expand, the attention of committees, subcommittees, and devoted individual members is inevitably spread thinner and thinner.

Partly because of the incapacity of the Congress to cope with an expanding Government, the line separating executive from legislative power has been shifted in favor of the Executive. In part, this shift has been made with congressional consent: the Congress has willingly and repeatedly delegated power to the Executive. Thus it has recognized, in the case of price and wage controls, that measures to curb inflation must be left to executive discretion. Similarly, major decisions to cope with the energy crisis have been delegated. In other cases, the shift has occurred without express congressional consent but with its acquiescence. In foreign affairs, much of what used to be done through treaties, which require ratification by the Senate, is now done through executive agreements, which do not. Above all, the effective power to declare war, which was granted to the Congress by the Constitution in clearest terms, has passed to the President. Even after Vietnam the Congress has not seriously considered taking back the power to put the country into war; it has only required that after the President has done so, he submit his decision for approval.

The Congress has yet to accept any general principle that the President should be free to impound appropriated funds, but it has repeatedly let Presidents do so without rebuke, providing the precedent and the encouragement for President Nixon to go further in this direction than any of his predecessors. Indeed, while congressmen have protested the President's impoundment of appropriated funds, in 1972 both houses voted to grant him broad authority to do exactly that. One day, it can confidently be predicted, the power to adjust tax rates within defined limits will also pass to the President so that fiscal policy can be "fine tuned" to cope with inflationary or recessionary trends.

Congressional checks also have been weakened by the trend toward secrecy, with claims of executive privilege and "national security" extending ever lower into the executive branch. The courts are now reviewing the scope of what can be withheld from Congress and from the courts themselves, and some retreat on the part of the President may be forced. But it is difficult to imagine that the long-term trend toward increasing secrecy will be decisively reversed.

Despite demands that the Congress "reassert" itself, there has been no action yet that would rectify the imbalance even to a slight degree. And it is difficult to see how the balance can be shifted much. The Government is not going to become smaller or easier for the Congress to oversee. The speed with which domestic and foreign problems arise and grow is not going to slow down even to the pace of a Congress aroused and streamlined, should that ideal condition ever be attained. Diplomacy will continue to be carried on as every other country carries it on: by the Executive in secret. The Congress cannot control inflation or cope with energy shortages or establish tariffs except through delegation of authority to the Executive. The presidential rights of impoundment and executive privilege may be curtailed a little, but that is about all. Even with the fullest "reassertion" of its powers, the Congress cannot reassert authority it has never had: Its powers will remain those of a confirming body before the fact, and a reviewing body after the fact, with no means of preventing the abuse of executive power when it is taking place.

The Decline of the Cabinet

If presidential power has been suddenly aggrandized, it is not only because power has flowed laterally from the Con-

gress but also because it has flowed upward from the Cabinet.
The decline of the authority of cabinet members has been
perhaps the most fundamental of all the forces affecting
the power balance in the national Government.

In the early days of the Republic, the Cabinet usually included the principal leaders of the President's party and
covered the spectrum of the party's composition. Presidents
often named to their Cabinets men who had been their
principal rivals for the party's nomination. Prominent members of the Senate were commonly appointed, along with
political leaders from the major states. Men like Clay and
Calhoun, Webster and Seward, Sherman and Bryan sat in
presidential Cabinets because they had independent power
bases that demanded, or deserved, recognition. And Cabinets
were used as consultative bodies. Presidents could still ignore
or overrule them, of course. Lincoln could say, "Seven noes
and one aye; the ayes have it." But at least he asked for his
Cabinet's opinion, and he took a vote.

Now, all this has changed. Replacing the Cabinet as the
President's consultative group has been a presidential-level
staff composed of appointees who have no outside power
bases and hence no independence. This staff formulates
policy for the President, issues orders on his behalf, and
supervises and coordinates their execution. It has enabled
the President to assume *command* of the executive branch
in a sense that is truly military. As in an army, so in the
executive branch it is now the headquarters staff that de-
cides; the Cabinet officers, reduced to the status of field com-
manders, execute.

In the old days, the President had to rely on his Cabinet;
its members were all he had to run the Government with.
Now, with his modern management apparatus, the President need no longer even talk with them. Nor has he time.
No President since Eisenhower has used the Cabinet even as
a consultative body. It meets pro forma, if at all, as a convenient way for the President to give pep talks and issue
instructions. With the Cabinet's decline in status has come

an inevitable change in the character of its members. The nineteenth century tradition that the President appoint strong political leaders with independent power bases has withered away—a trend that has reached a kind of culmination in the present Administration.

The last thing an ambitious presidential staff wants is department heads with independent power bases. Such men have the strength to be defiant and cause trouble. What such a White House staff wants is, in the words of one former Nixon aide, men "who will, when the White House orders them to jump, only ask 'how high?'" To make doubly sure that department heads would be compliant, the White House has systematically placed in subcabinet positions, as under secretaries or in lesser posts, trusted political and White House aides.

But the flow of power from the departments to the presidency, like the shift in the congressional-presidential balance, has not been the product of pure willfulness. Here, too, the trend has had a basis in the realities of modern government. The executive branch does need central direction and coordination; it cannot be treated as a cluster of independent satrapies, each responsive only to its clientele. There must be a coordinated budget. Departments do have to respond to common policies established by officials responsible to the people through elective processes—and the only such official in the executive branch is the President. These needs, too, are affected by the great complexity, the faster tempo, and the closer interrelationships among governmental activities. In domestic fields, as in war and diplomacy, the Government must be able to marshal its resources and act decisively and consistently whether the battle is against inflation or pollution, a recession or an energy shortage.

The answer to the problem of misused presidential power is not to try to disperse the essential components of that power among semi-independent agencies within the executive branch. That would only reintroduce the problems of conflict and administrative weakness that compelled the centralization of power in the first place. Besides being unwise, such an approach would be essentially unenforceable. The Congress could probably find ways, through its appropriation power, to reduce somewhat the size of the White House and Executive Office staffs, but the Congress has shown no wish to interfere with a President's way of doing business to the point of trying to dismantle the presidential office. Short of such a step, there is no way to enforce a new set of President–Cabinet relations. A President can hardly be compelled to appoint strong and independent political figures to the Cabinet and to repose power in them if he prefers to rely on White House aides. The organization of the executive branch is, by its nature, an executive function.

Did the Founding Fathers Err?

If the power of the presidency cannot be reduced very much—and if, in a fast-moving and complex world, it probably should not be—then how does one solve the basic problem of too much power in one man? I suggest that most current analysis of the problem has been misdirected because it concentrates on the first three words of that phrase: *too much power.* I submit that the solution is to be found by looking instead at the last three words: *in one man.*

An institutional principle applied almost universally in the English-speaking world is that major decisions should be made not by one man acting alone, but by a collective body of some kind. In the United States, legislatures are all plural bodies. So are juries, the higher courts, and the regulatory commissions. Corporations and voluntary-service organizations, school systems and universities are run by plural boards of directors who select and supervise the managers. In political parties the ultimate authority lies in conventions and committees. The one great exception to this principle is the executive branch of the United States Government (along with the executive branches of the state governments and some city governments that are patterned after it).

In other English-speaking countries, even such exceptions do not exist. Executive power rests in plural cabinets, as it does in most non-English-speaking democracies as well. Even in the nondemocracies, power is often lodged at least formally in plural bodies such as the Politburo in the Soviet Union.

This pattern is not accidental. Rather, it embodies a wisdom that has evolved over centuries of experience with human organization. Societies have learned again and again that to entrust power to one man is inherently dangerous. He may be erratic or impulsive or obsessive in his judgments, or arbitrary and unfair. He may be incompetent, a bungler. He may be lazy, negligent, or corrupt. He may pervert the ends of the organization for his own benefit, whether to gain money or punish enemies or reward friends, or simply to perpetuate himself and his followers in office. Hence, in almost every organization the restraint of collective decision making is forced upon the leader. He is made subordinate to, or required to act as a member of, a plural body of some kind. It may be called by many names—commission, council, board, committee, senate, house, cabinet —but its members have a degree of independence of the leader.

Plural decision making has its own drawbacks, obviously. It can cause delay, undue caution, and resistance to innovation. Those who seek spectacular progressivism are more likely to find it in presidents and governors than in congresses and legislatures, for the single leader can march without having to be in lockstep with anyone. But the experience of centuries has weighed the disadvantage against the merits and given its verdict—that the plural body, not the single leader, is better to be trusted. When a single executive is needed to dispatch the execution of a collective body's policy, he is made responsible to and is supervised by that body. Never is he left free to act unchecked, responsible only to the general membership of the organization and to himself.

If this be the folk wisdom, one must ponder how the Founding Fathers came to stray so far. They were sensitive to the danger of concentrating power in any institution, but in their day it was the prospect of too much power in the legislature that concerned them most. They feared that in a republic, the majority of the legislature would get out of hand and threaten the rights of the minority—and their fear seemed borne out by the experience of the states in the decade before the Constitutional Convention. As men of property, they feared the mob, the levelers. So the question was whether the President would be strong enough. Nevertheless, the vote for a one-man presidency was not unanimous. The Convention debated whether the head of the executive branch should be one man or three; seven states preferred the single executive, three states the plural. Had the Founders foreseen how the system of presidential election they designed would change—how the power of selection would pass from a judicious electoral college made up of leading citizens to a popular process resting largely on the vote of citizens in primary and general elections— one can wonder what the vote on a plural presidency would have been.

OVERPOWERING THE CONSTITUTION? [3]

The uniquely powerful nature of the modern presidency is not yet fully understood, even though the near reverence people have tended to feel for it has been shaken by recent crises. How many Americans are aware, for example, that a President on his own initiative can order a nuclear attack —but that not even the Soviet Union or China grants such ultimate discretionary authority to any one man? In those Communist countries a decision to begin a war that could end the world almost certainly would require the assent of the party leaders.

The awesome powers now in the hands of Richard Nixon

[3] Article by Morton Mintz, a national reporter for the Washington *Post*; co-author of *America, Inc.: Who Owns and Operates the United States. Newsweek.* 82:15. N. 12, '73. Copyright Newsweek, Inc., 1973, reprinted by permission.

—and before him in the hands of Lyndon Johnson and John Kennedy—were acquired under a Constitution that, ironically, was designed to maintain a balance of powers among supposedly coequal branches of Government. Yet, not much attention is given to the role of the Constitution or to its adequacy and appropriateness today.

Perhaps the explanation is that we have been stunned by revelations that suggest a need to rethink the Constitution while depriving us of an atmosphere for contemplation. We learn that a President—our President—waged secret wars. We find that a series of lawless acts—burglaries, wiretappings, obstructions of justice—have been committed in the name of "national security." Crimes are covered up. The President's reelection organization is disclosed to have practiced polite extortion. The former attorney general and former secretary of commerce who headed that organization are indicted. There are near collisions with the courts. And the suspicion grows that a President who twice swore to uphold the Constitution has subverted its spirit and letter, especially the First and Fourth Amendments.

Excessive Power?

Should we not then be concerned about whether flaws in our Constitution have permitted excessive power to flow into the White House to begin with?

To take a principal case in point, we have no reliable, systematic way to hold a President accountable, short of the draconian remedy of impeachment.

He invokes executive privilege, a doctrine without constitutional sanction, to deny accountability in Congress and the courts. He invokes it, be it noted, even to impede congressional and court investigations of an apparent connection between a large campaign "contribution" by major milk producers and a subsequent increase in milk-price supports.

He asserts freedom *from* the press by treating it as suits his whim.

He is, in theory, accountable to the electorate, but only once in four years and not at all while serving a second term and barred from seeking a third.

The question should be faced whether a constitutional convention should be called. Some shudder at the mere mention of such an idea. They fear it would open the door to a new Constitution in which the spirit of freedom would be displaced by Yahoo prejudice. I, for one, am skeptical that such a disaster could occur, *provided*: that the delegates would be truly representative of the American people, and *provided* that they would have the opportunity to deliberate and reflect, for months if necessary, on what in the Constitution is precious and should be retained—certainly the Bill of Rights—and what should be modified, discarded, or replaced.

Convulsions

The Founding Fathers, after much debate, left the powers of the presidency deliberately vague. In the twentieth century, the office has become monarchical, as George Reedy demonstrated in his brilliant *The Twilight of the Presidency*, and as recent convulsions have confirmed.

A king may have many palaces; a President has lavish White Houses west and south, not to mention a luxurious retreat in Maryland. A king may surround himself with men who say, "Yes, your Majesty"; a President has courtiers who say, "Yes, Mr. President." A king of old asserted divine right; a President asserts executive privilege.

How could a President be made accountable? Could he be required to appear in Congress, frequently and regularly, to answer questions? Could a means be devised for the voter to pinpoint his contents and discontents? Should he be voting for attorney general and possibly other high offices, or should he pull a lever quadrennially only for President?

Should the office of Vice President be abolished, or should the means for choosing him be changed? What of the electoral college? Should the President be limited to two terms? Should the presidency be abandoned outright in favor of an elected council that would choose one of its members to be Chief of State? When all is said and done, would the best form of governance be basically what we have now?

To prevent tyranny, the Founding Fathers provided checks and balances on the centers of governmental power: the executive, the legislature, and the judiciary. A century passed before the Industrial Revolution evolved a crucial new power center: the giant—and, now, often multinational —corporations. The framers of the Constitution had no way of knowing that the corporations, interlocked with financial institutions, would come to rule us, just as surely as does the Government.

Corporations govern overtly by, say, levying taxes in the form of noncompetitive or monopolistic prices, by taking life through the provision of unsafe job sites, such as the coal mines have been through most of our history, and by polluting the air and waters.

Corporations rule covertly by governing the Government, the most obvious technique being election-campaign contributions (or investments) that make politicians beholden. So feeble are our checks and balances that private governments such as ITT and international oil companies have representation without taxation.

Is It "a Person"?

Surely a constitutional convention would want to examine the power of the megacorporation which, under a Supreme Court decision of a century ago, is a "person." Is it?

The two hundredth anniversary of our country comes in 1976. How better could we observe it than with a constitutional convention? But Congress probably won't move to call one, being itself, to a disheartening extent, an assemblage of petty sovereigns often neglectful of the welfare of the citizenry while preoccupied with the welfare of special interests: defense contractors, highway builders, banks, oil companies, milk producers and large corporations generally.

Even so, there is no inhibition on the calling of a mock constitutional convention. Admittedly, it would serve a purely educational function. But that could be a valuable undertaking for the nation as it enters its third century.

IMAGE AND MEDIA [4]

A powerful case exists against American television and the press, but Richard Nixon and his men are forever getting it wrong. It is not that the media are hostile to Presidents, and to Nixon more than most, but that they are such abject tools so eager to be of presidential use that they have distorted all our perceptions of what news is and what Government is about.

Some years ago, I was assigned to the White House for the Baltimore *Sun* and as a lean, untempered rookie went with President Eisenhower to vacation in the western air. Vacationing was a big part of White House coverage in those days, and Eisenhower did it thoroughly. For five and six weeks at a time he did absolutely nothing remotely definable as news.

Each day, however, my more professional colleagues would unsheath their typewriters, pound away for an hour or two and wire home stories. It was not a little disconcerting to a new boy when, after four or five days without having sent a word, I found the veterans joking about how long I could go on reporting nothing from the Rockies and stay on the payroll.

The President, I quickly learned, is always news, whether he is involved in any news or not. So we all poured out reams of material daily. The President had eaten beef bacon and skim milk at breakfast, we told America. He had risen at 6:30 and fished. He had talked on the telephone.

[4] "The Mediums," article by Russell Baker, staff columnist. New York *Times Magazine*. p 4. Ap. 7, '74. © 1974 by The New York Times Company. Reprinted by permission.

He had enjoyed a good day on the golf course. He was in good spirits. Two businessmen had paid a courtesy call. He had played bridge.

It was worse than nonsense, of course, because it created a totally deceptive impression and, by keeping the President constantly in the "news"—for this drivel was published and broadcast extensively through the country—it distorted the public's perception of Government, leaving the notion that the President, like the planet Jupiter, was a force constantly in motion.

Nothing has changed significantly since then in the appetite of both press and television for presidential "news." On any given evening, the top "news" items on the network shows will concern the President. On a typical day, the New York *Times* front page will display two or three stories from the White House. President Nixon has declared, or rejected, or challenged, or stated, or flown, or worked on, or met with, or released, or issued, or signed, or smiled, or looked tense.

And how often is it news? Very rarely. Most often it is, in Daniel Boorstin's splendid phrase, a "pseudo event"; that is, an event created to satisfy the media's ceaseless craving for something—anything—to be reported.

Such was President Nixon's recent flurry of television appearances in news conferences around the country. In the typical presidential news conference no news occurs. It is staged because cameras are available and editors have space at hand from which they are always willing to clear real, but dull, news about the nuts, bolts and boring percentage points of real government for sure-fire hokum about the President.

Typically, the stories produced by these pseudo events deal heavily in how he looked, whether the audience was friendly and how well he performed under pressure. They are in the main exercises in the aggrandizement of fatuity.

The ease with which Nixon has exploited these lazy old media habits with his recent series of pseudo events must make a logical mind wonder why he chose to wage that self-destructive war upon them? When they were so deferential, so willing to be of service in the glorification of his office, where was the gain in the niggling quarrel with a handful of reporters, small voices in the storm, who occasionally tried interposing themselves between him and the picture of glory their papers and networks were painting of his office?

Well, he wanted total complaisance, of course. *Media*—dreadful word—is an advertising term; it implies the use of television and newspapers for ads that sell goods; television and newspapers do not argue with their ads. The Nixon people wanted no argument with theirs. After the President had used television to sell, he wanted no reporters following him immediately afterward to discuss the message.

In this insistence on reducing the media to the humiliating status of advertising media, this demand to have everything presented absolutely his way when he already had all the riches the media could bestow upon mortal man, he was like a sultan fuming because there were gnats on the bananas.

They still serve him well. If you think not, check this paper's news columns and see how much declaring, announcing, meeting and conferring he did only yesterday.

THE EXECUTIVE GRIP ON JOBS [5]

After little more than four years in office, the Nixon Administration, through the use of appointments and other means, has turned the independent regulatory agencies into bastions of Nixon Republicanism.

They are run by members and commissioners who generally share the President's philosophy for less interference with business and industry. And they have less diversity than existed in the past, with academics, liberals and consumer activists in short supply.

[5] "Nixon's Imprint Is Deep at Regulatory Agencies," article by John Herbers, of the New York *Times* Washington Bureau. New York *Times*. p 1+. My. 5, '73. © 1973 by The New York Times Company. Reprinted by permission.

It has been traditional for Presidents to shape the agencies in accordance with their own goals and political ideas. But the Nixon White House, in the view of a wide range of authorities interviewed during the last few weeks, has gone further than other recent Administrations.

Indicative is President Nixon's appointment last March 12 [1973] of Lee R. West, a little-known state district judge of Ada, Oklahoma, to the Civil Aeronautics Board and the controversy it set off.

The Senate Commerce Committee is holding up Mr. West's confirmation because committee leaders wanted the post to go to Robert T. Murphy, a consumer-oriented board member whose twelve-year term has been marked by votes for more airline competition and against mergers and who was a candidate for reappointment.

A Corporate Constituent

Instead, the White House chose Mr. West, whose name had been submitted by Senator Henry R. Bellmon, Republican of Oklahoma, with the support of House Speaker Carl Albert, a Democrat, also of Oklahoma.

The two Oklahomans share as a corporate constituent American Airlines, which was disappointed at the board's refusal last year to grant a merger between American and Western airlines. American officials have said publicly they want Mr. Murphy replaced.

Yet so strong is the tradition of giving the President a free hand in regulatory appointments, senators say, that it is probably only a matter of time before the committee yields and Mr. West takes his seat on the five-member board. Mr. Murphy, whose term expired January 1, is serving in the interim.

With the expected departure of Mr. Murphy and of Federal Communications Commission member Nicholas Johnson, whose term runs out in June, Nixon appointees will so predominate on the major regulatory agencies that the stinging dissents that have come from holdovers from previous Administrations are expected to be a thing of the past.

Arms of Congress

The boards and commissions were originally set up as arms of Congress to regulate and formulate policy in broad areas of trade, transportation and communications. To make them as independent as possible, Congress provided that the members have staggered terms and that they represent both political parties.

However, the agencies rarely have been independent of either Congress or the White House, and some students of government do not think they should be. In recent years, under both Democratic and Republican Administrations, there has been more control of the agencies by the President, or more often by his assistants. The agencies are not ordinarily a matter of high presidential priority.

Kenneth C. Davis, a professor of administrative law at the University of Chicago, who advised President Kennedy on his regulatory appointments, maintains that there is not a great deal of difference between the regulatory bodies, which are supposed to be independent, and the administrative agencies and departments, which are run by the President.

"Congress still prefers independence and the President still prefers to have subordinates," he said in a telephone interview. "The reality is not that different. The difference is much less than people expect."

Influence Held Increasing

The staggered terms rarely work to prevent a President from gaining control due to frequent resignations that arise from various pressures and the tradition that the chairmen serve at the pleasure of the President. Of 38 positions on six major regulatory bodies—the Civil Aeronautics Board, the Federal Communications Commission, the Federal Power

Commission, the Federal Trade Commission, the Interstate Commerce Commission and the Securities and Exchange Commission—President Nixon, after little more than four years in office, has filled 28, including the reappointments and those not yet confirmed. He has named the chairmen of all six.

According to congressional testimony and a number of officials and regulatory experts interviewed over the last few weeks, presidential influence has increased in some areas under Mr. Nixon.

His appointments have represented less of an ideological mix than those of previous Presidents. For example, he appointed Alfred T. MacFarland, a Tennessee lawyer, as a Democrat to the Interstate Commerce Commission under the requirement that no more than a bare majority of members be of the same party.

The Senate Commerce Commission balked at the appointment, contending that, even though Mr. MacFarland might be known as a Democrat back in Tennessee, he had a long record of supporting Republican candidates. The White House then had Mr. MacFarland change his registration to independent and resubmitted the nomination.

"We could do nothing but confirm him," said Senator Frank E. Moss, Democrat of Utah. "I don't like it, but I couldn't help but have some admiration for the bold way they did it."

Budgetary control over the agencies by the executive branch, which has existed for a number of years, has increased under the Nixon Administration, according to testimony taken last year by the Senate Subcommittee on Intergovernmental Relations of the Committee on Government Operations.

The Office of Management and Budget, a White House agency, has included some of the regulatory agencies in Administrationwide expenditure and personnel cuts ordered by the President. This, according to Senator Edward J. Gurney, Republican of Florida—who is an Administra-

tion supporter—was "sort of a new and far-reaching authority that either did not exist or was not used before."

POWER PARADOX [6]

The energy policy debate shifts now to Senate-House
conferees; energy chief William E. Simon [now Secretary
of the Treasury] urges legislators not to tie his hands.

"Flexibility" is stressed by Mr. Simon—flexibility for his
Federal Energy Office to move swiftly to combat shortages
as they crop up "across the whole barrel of oil," from crude
to gasoline.

An emergency-powers bill passed by the Senate November 19 [1973] grants the White House the broad authority
sought by President Nixon and Mr. Simon, including the
power to ration gasoline.

But the House version of the bill, passed December 15,
subjects gasoline rationing to congressional veto and
requires specific Senate and House approval, through the
normal legislative process, of a range of other conservation
measures.

Measure of Authority

Under the Senate bill, for example, Mr. Nixon could
order changes in working hours, set national speed limits,
curtail outdoor lighting, and define maximum thermostat
settings. The House version would oblige him to seek congressional approval of such steps.

Mr. Simon, after discussing the House-passed measure
with the President, said the White House "could not tol-
erate" the House bill's "impediments" to swift emergency
action.

The President joined his energy chief in urging Senate
and House conferees to work out an acceptable compromise
bill and hand it to Mr. Nixon for signing before the

[6] "Simon: We Must Act Fast," article by Harry B. Ellis, business-financial
correspondent of The Christian Science Monitor. Christian Science Monitor.
p 1+. D. 17, '73. Reprinted by permission from The Christian Science Monitor.
© 1973 The Christian Science Publishing Society. All rights reserved.

Christmas recess. [The Senate version of the bill was the one enacted.—Ed.]

Rationing Complexity

Differing language on gasoline rationing is not what primarily troubles the White House, for the President and his top economic advisers oppose gasoline rationing, except as a last resort. Rationing, says Mr. Simon, is still "last on his list."

With "123 million licensed American drivers and 108 million cars in service," noted Mr. Simon on the CBS-TV program "Face the Nation" . . . , equitable gasoline rationing becomes immensely complex.

Across-the-board rationing, based on present supply projections, might allow ten gallons weekly per American. But there would be exceptions, declared the energy chief. The people of Los Angeles, as one example, "can only get to work by car."

In a related move, President Nixon signed into law a bill putting the United States on daylight saving time for nearly two years, beginning at 2 A.M. on January 6 [1974] when the nation's clocks will be advanced by one hour. The move could save the equivalent of 150,000 barrels of oil daily, according to the White House.

IV. WAR POWERS

EDITOR'S INTRODUCTION

From a legal standpoint there have been three key constitutional issues involved in all the recent jousting between the Congress and the executive branch under President Nixon. They are executive privilege, the impoundment of funds, and the question of war powers. Of the three, the question of war powers has been the most crucial. It is for that reason, perhaps, that Congress has acted most resolutely on it.

This section examines the separation of war powers and traces how Congress reasserted its right over that issue. The first article is by Senator Ervin of North Carolina, the chief figure in the Congress's battle to regain its constitutional powers. Senator Ervin looks at the separation of powers in the conduct of foreign affairs. The conduct of war is, of course, an inseparable part of that issue. The next article, from the *Congressional Quarterly Almanac*, considers the granting of "emergency powers" to the President. These powers form the legal basis for US involvement in Vietnam, that is, the Tonkin Gulf Resolution.

The third item is a news analysis from the *National Observer* published in July 1973. Earlier in the year the public at large had learned that the United States had been carrying on a secret air war against Communists in Cambodia. Thousands of air missions had been flown. But even Congress was unaware of them because the Pentagon and the White House had kept them secret with false record keeping. The article describes the revelations and tells how Congress finally forced a halt to the bombings. It also notes that Congress readied laws that would strongly limit a

President's ability to wage war without congressional approval. On this point, the news analysis was not hopeful; President Nixon said that he would veto the bill and the newspaper's tally indicated that there were not enough votes to override his veto.

But suprising events do occur. The next news story, from the Washington *Post*, describes how the Congress overrode a presidential veto and enacted legislation to limit his ability to wage war. The final article in the section, a short editorial from the New York *Times*, assesses the impact of the bill's passage on the power battle between Congress and the Executive and concludes that Congress is winning back some of the power that the Constitution intended it to have.

THE CONSTITUTIONAL CHARGES [1]

When the delegates to the Constitutional Convention gathered in Philadelphia in 1787 to draft a Constitution for the new American republic, they were almost universally determined to circumscribe the authority of the Executive with respect to foreign affairs. The virtually limitless power of the English Crown over foreign affairs and its consequences were very much on the minds of our Founding Fathers.

To limit executive authority over foreign affairs and over other matters delegated to the Federal Government by the Constitution, the drafters devised and incorporated into the Constitution the principle of separation of powers. Recent developments in the field of foreign affairs notwithstanding, it is as clear as the noonday sun in a cloudless sky that the Constitution divides the National Government's foreign-affairs powers between the Congress and the President, granting to neither such exclusive control that one can be effective without cooperation from the other.

[1] "The Separation of Powers," article by Senator Sam J. Ervin, Jr. (Democrat, North Carolina). *Center Magazine*. p 8+. Ja./F. '74. Reprinted with permission from the January/February, 1974, issue of *The Center Magazine*, a publication of the Center for the Study of Democratic Institutions, Santa Barbara, California.

Unfortunately some persons, both in government and in academia, have so little regard for the principle of separation of powers as to embrace the notion that the "realities" of modern international affairs require almost exclusive executive control over foreign policy. They contend that arbitrary executive control of America's foreign affairs is the price of survival in this uncertain, nuclear age.

I agree that the political, economic, and technological changes over the last fifty years necessitate changes in the institutions and processes by which our foreign policy is formulated and implemented. But I do not agree that we must abandon constitutional principles, especially the principle of separation of powers, which have served us so well throughout our history. Our constitutional form of government was designed not only to make government feasible and practical but also to guard against the historic temptation and irresistible urge of those who govern to gather and use limitless power over the governed.

I believe that the primary responsibility for the determination of substantive foreign policy rests with the Congress and that the President is obliged to administer that policy within the framework established by the Congress. According to my reading of the Constitution and constitutional history, the President's role in foreign affairs is primarily representative and instrumental. Not one syllable in the Constitution or one word of verified historical evidence supports the view that the President has broad discretion to act without the collaboration and consent of the Congress in foreign affairs.

The document drafted and ratified as our fundamental instrument of government by these freedom-loving Americans demonstrates conclusively, if not always quite exactly, that the Congress was intended to have significant and sometimes singular powers with respect to the foreign affairs of the National Government. Article I gives to the Congress the power to "regulate commerce with foreign nations"—historically the basis for American foreign policy. It allocates to Congress the power to "provide for the common defense," "declare war," "raise and support armies," "provide and maintain a navy," "make rules for the government and regulation of the land and naval forces," and other powers directly related to the making of foreign policy and the conduct of foreign affairs.

Furthermore, in granting to Congress "all legislative powers" and the power over appropriations, the Constitution places in the collective hands of Congress such enormous power as to make the effective creation and implementation of foreign policy impossible without congressional cooperation or, at least, acquiescence.

By contrast, the enumerated powers of the President with respect to foreign affairs, set forth in Article II, are few and not as comprehensive, at least on their face. According to Article II, the President is "Commander-in-Chief of the Army and Navy of the United States." He is also therein granted the power—with advice and consent of the Senate—to make treaties and to appoint ambassadors and is authorized to "receive ambassadors and other public ministers." He has the duty to see that the laws are faithfully executed and commands whatever other powers may result from the vesting of "executive power" in the presidency.

Despite the documented desire of the Founding Fathers to prevent executive autonomy over foreign affairs and the Constitution's generous grants of power to the legislative branch in this field, developments over the past thirty to forty years have caused many students of American constitutional and political history to doubt that Congress can or should significantly participate in the development, establishment, and implementation of American foreign policy. Quite simply, many citizens have come to believe that American foreign relations are within the domain of the President.

While I agree that the Congress in fact has not exercised effectively its considerable powers in foreign affairs, I do not agree with the proposition that executive hegemony in this area is necessary or that it is an inevitable result of changing historical circumstances to be accepted despite clear constitutional principles to the contrary. Indeed, I share the strongly held view of the Founding Fathers that, in the area of foreign affairs more than any other, the principle of the separation of powers is essential to our republican form of government.

For Congress to reassert its proper role as a full partner in foreign affairs, Congress and the public must come to appreciate what has caused the erosion of legislative effectiveness in this field.

One of the problems is the nature of foreign affairs itself and the consequential impact of the Constitution's division of foreign-affairs powers. The Constitution has divided between the legislative and executive branches what is almost an indivisible process. Congressional power to declare war and the President's powers as Commander-in-Chief, for instance, affect each other so directly that it is impossible for either branch to exercise these powers effectively without the active cooperation or passive acquiescence of the other. And without congressional willingness to appropriate the funds needed to implement foreign policy— designed with or without congressional consultation—no policy can be effective. Thus, what the Congress and the President can and cannot do constitutionally in foreign affairs has been in issue since George Washington's presidency, in part because of the practical indivisibility of the National Government's power over foreign affairs.

Another problem is the somewhat vague and incomplete constitutional language with respect to the granting and separating of foreign-affairs powers. If one adopted a very narrow interpretation of the constitutional language, there would be many decision-making processes and functions granted to neither the Congress nor the President. And, while the theory of inherent, sovereign power may supply a reasonable basis for describing the total scope of the National Government's foreign-affairs power, such a theory is no help in determining whether these unenumerated inherent functions and processes belong to the Congress or to the President.

The Constitution vests all legislative powers in the Congress and all executive powers in the President, but this division is inadequate by itself to determine which of the two branches has exclusive or concurrent authority with respect to a particular foreign-affairs function not expressly provided for in the Constitution. Even where the Constitution explicitly grants one branch a foreign-affairs power, confusion and conflict have arisen when the other branch asserts a reasonable claim to a related, unenumerated power. This particular difficulty has been manifested in the use of armed force by the President in circumstances "less than war," while only the Congress has the power to declare a war.

Another difficulty has resulted from Congress's delegating vast authority over foreign affairs to the President during the last several decades. Generally, Congress has not only the right but a constitutional duty to set standards for the exercise of delegated authority and it can withdraw such authority at any time. In foreign affairs, however, these delegations of power to the President usually have been made with few if any standards, and Congress has rarely reviewed presidential execution of these delegated powers. In my opinion Congress's practice of giving to the President power over foreign affairs without understandable and effective guidelines and effective congressional oversight has clouded the constitutional issue of separation of powers and has seriously undermined Congress's capacity to participate in the making of foreign policy.

The Senate Foreign Relations committee said in 1967: "The concentration in the hands of the President of virtually unlimited authority over matters of war and peace has all but removed the limits to executive power in the most important single area of our national life. Until they are restored, the American people will be threatened with tyranny or disaster."

Today's ascendancy of presidential power over foreign affairs was clearly not intended by the Founding Fathers. It has no constitutional basis; and it threatens the capacity of the National Government to formulate and execute a foreign policy which represents the best interests of our people. Theories devised to justify comprehensive executive authority over foreign affairs do not rely on the words of the Constitution which, according to Professor Edward Corwin, do no more than ". . . confer on the President certain powers capable of affecting our foreign relations, and certain other powers of the same general kind on the Senate, and still other such powers on Congress. . . ."

We cannot look to the third branch, the judiciary, for a revitalization of the doctrine of separation of powers in the field of foreign affairs. Since the adoption of our Constitution, the Supreme Court has had very few occasions to interpret and apply that doctrine in foreign affairs. The opinion written by Mr. Justice Sutherland in the 1936 case, *United States v. Curtiss-Wright Export Corp.*, 299 U.S. 304—the most celebrated Supreme Court decision in this area—confounds more than it clarifies. Justice Sutherland's statement that "the investment of the Federal Government with the powers of external sovereignty did not depend upon the affirmative grants of the Constitution," 299 U.S. 304 (315), signals great confusion as to understanding the Constitution's division of these foreign-affairs powers between the executive and legislative branches. The judicial concept of justiciability and the ultimate political nature of this problem no doubt will continue to preclude the courts from offering effective or definitive answers to the questions which must be met.

The burden of restoring separation of powers in foreign affairs rests directly on the shoulders of Congress. This great principle of government can be revived only if and when the Congress asserts its rightful authority in formulating, implementing, and reviewing American foreign policy.

The legislative branch may now be awakening to its constitutional duties and its opportunities in foreign affairs.

In recent years, many bills have been introduced in the Congress to correct the present imbalance of power between the two branches. I do not subscribe to each of these legislative proposals, but their introduction and the broad support they receive indicates an intensified congressional determination that the legislative branch assume its proper constitutional role in foreign affairs.

One particular abuse of executive power in the area of foreign affairs with which I have been especially concerned as chairman of the Senate Subcommittee on Separation of Powers is the use of so-called executive agreements to circumvent the treaty-making provisions of the Constitution. Article II, Section 2, of the Constitution states that the President ". . . shall have power, by and with the advice and consent of the Senate, to make treaties, provided two-thirds of the senators present concur." The Senate is thereby given at least a "veto" over commitments made by this country pursuant to a treaty with another country. On the other hand, the Constitution does not expressly grant to the President any power to enter executive agreements.

The Constitution does not mention the term *executive agreement*, and there is no accepted definition of what constitutes an executive agreement.

The legal basis for the use of executive agreements is unclear at best. Most frequently it has been grounded on the argument of "usage"—a legal justification not entirely satisfactory. As I have noted in various other contexts, murder and rape have been with us since the dawn of human history, but that fact does not make rape legal or murder meritorious. In effect, reliance on "usage" in this instance grounds concepts of constitutionality on acquiescence rather than on the written document, and that, to my mind, is wholly unacceptable.

There has been a considerable, and I would say unfortunate, increase in the use of executive agreements as an instrument of American foreign policy in the past few decades. As recently as 1930, the United States concluded twenty-five treaties and only nine executive agreements. In 1968, the United States concluded sixteen treaties and 266 executive agreements. By January 1, 1972, the United States had a total of 947 treaties and 4,359 executive agreements. This suggests that significant decisions affecting American foreign policy are being made by the executive branch without effective congressional participation. The executive agreement may be a legitimate method for the President to carry out foreign policy established jointly by the President and the Congress. The extensive use made of this instrument in recent years, however, demonstrates that it is being used not only for administrative convenience but also, intended or not, to circumvent the Congress as an equal partner in the making of foreign policy.

To reduce the trend of bypassing the Congress in the making of international agreements and to implement the spirit of Article II, Section 2, of the Constitution, I have introduced legislation which would provide for congressional review of executive agreements.

The bill, S. 1472, is simple in its terms. It recognizes that the Founding Fathers' concept of shared powers in the area of international agreements has been substantially eroded by the use of executive agreements. In plain language, the measure defines executive agreements and requires that the Secretary of State shall transmit each such agreement to both houses of Congress. If, in the opinion of the President, the disclosure of any such agreement would be prejudicial to the security of the United States, the bill provides that it shall be transmitted to the Commitee on Foreign Relations of the Senate and the Committee on Foreign Affairs of the House of Representatives under an appropriate injunction of secrecy which would permit only the members of both houses of the Congress to inspect the document.

The bill further provides that each executive agreement transmitted to the Congress shall come into force and be made effective after sixty days—or later if the agreement so provides—unless both houses pass a concurrent resolution expressing disapproval of the executive agreement between the date it is transmitted to the Congress and the end of a sixty-day period. In other words, the Congress, in its shared-power role, will have an opportunity to state that it does not approve of an executive agreement during the sixty-day period after the agreement is transmitted to the Congress. [With some modification the bill was passed over the President's veto. See "New Curbs on War," below in this section.—Ed.]

It appears to me that the executive branch of the Government would welcome a method whereby the Congress would share the responsibility for making international agreements which affect the international image of our nation and its people, the allocation of our tax resources, and, in many instances the possibilities of achieving peace in the world.

EMERGENCY POWERS [2]

The Historical Background

The United States had been living under a declared state of national emergency for the past forty years, and in 1973 there were in existence four states of national emergency, according to the Special Senate Committee on the Termination of the National Emergency. The committee recommended all four be terminated. They were:

Roosevelt Proclamation. Immediately after his inauguration on March 4, 1933, President Franklin D. Roosevelt declared that a national emergency existed as a result of the economic crisis of the Depression. Congress March 9 ratified the President's declaration and amended the 1917 Trading With the Enemy Act to give him broad economic powers.

Truman Proclamation. On December 16, 1950, President Harry S Truman declared that a national emergency existed as a result of Communist aggression in Korea and in other

[2] "National Emergency Powers." *Congressional Quarterly Almanac.* 29:778-9. '73. Reprinted by permission.

parts of the world. He proclaimed it necessary for the United States to strengthen its defenses to repel threats to US security and to meet responsibilities to the United Nations.

Nixon Proclamations. On March 23, 1970, President Richard M. Nixon declared a national emergency had resulted from a postal service strike and ordered Federal troops to postal duty in New York.

President Nixon declared another national emergency on August 15, 1971, because of the international monetary crisis and imposed a surcharge on dutiable imports.

Interim Report

The Special Senate Committee on the Termination of the National Emergency issued an interim report September 30 [1973].

Highlighting four existing states of national emergencies it said should be ended, the committee released a catalog of some 470 existing emergency statutes which remain "a potential source of virtually unlimited power for a President should he choose to activate them," according to the committee.

The report and a compilation of the 470 laws the committee identified as delegating emergency powers to the President constituted the first phase of the committee's activities, after which it intended to complete a study of executive orders and to issue legislative recommendations. The committee, established early in 1973, was directed to make its final report by February 28, 1974.

The panel said there was a need for retention of essential powers for potential emergencies, but called for congressional participation in decisions to activate the powers and congressional review of the use of the powers. Committee cochairman Frank Church (Democrat, Idaho) called the recommendations "a long step back to constitutional government."

Powers. Presidential powers included the right to seize property, organize and control the means of production,

seize commodities, assign military forces abroad, call re-
serve forces amounting to 2.5 million men to duty, institute
martial law, seize and control all means of transportation,
regulate all private enterprise and restrict travel. These
statutory authorities were placed at the Executive's disposal
by presidential declarations of national emergencies in
1933, 1950, 1970 and 1971.

The 1917 Trading With the Enemy Act—giving the
President power to regulate transactions in foreign exchange, the export or hoarding of gold or silver coins or
bullion or currency and the transfers of credit in any form
between the United States and any foreign country—was
cited, during a September 28 [1973] press conference held
by Church and cochairman Charles McCurdy Mathias Jr.
(Republican, Maryland), as among the most important
emergency statutes. Also pointed out was the Feed and
Forage Act, an 1861 statute the Administration in 1972 said
could be used to fund US activities in Southeast Asia if
Congress failed to appropriate funds.

Other statutes highlighted by the committee included a
provision permitting the President to give military assistance to any foreign country and another which provided
the basis for the internment of Japanese-Americans in World
War II. A similar statute, the Emergency Detention Act,
was repealed by Congress in 1971.

   We cannot stress enough the warning contained in this
catalog of emergency powers statutes. The evident pattern in this
accretion of power over a forty-year period is, in our view, symp-
tomatic of what has occurred in lawmaking in all areas of our
Government [Church and Mathias said in a joint statement].
Unless Congress takes steps to strengthen its capacity to write the
laws through the representative political process as the Constitution intended, then the unmistakable drift toward one-man
government will continue.

Congressional Acquiescence. Throughout its review of
these statutes, the committee said it saw a consistent pattern
of lawmaking—one in which Congress transferred "awe-

some magnitudes of power" to the Executive to govern during crises. This transfer of authority was sharply criticized by the committee.

> The record of congressional performance is a poor one [Church and Mathias stated]. These laws—in the main, drafted in the executive branch—were passed hastily without much consideration. Almost all of the laws made no provision for congressional oversight nor do they provide a means for terminating the "temporary" delegated powers.

As an example, the committee cited the congressional reaction to Roosevelt's 1933 emergency proclamation. Within five days, a committee had approved ratification of the proclamation and amended a section of the 1917 Trading With the Enemy Act to extend to the President broad economic powers which had previously been limited to wartime. There was a total of eight hours of debate on the proposal in both houses, according to the committee.

The panel said that "this pattern of hasty and inadequate consideration" had been repeated during World War II, the Korean War and most recently during debate on the Tonkin Gulf Resolution in 1964.

Executive Orders. After completing its catalog of emergency power statutes, the committee began an examination of executive orders issued pursuant to these statutes. Church and Mathias reported: "The results of its study of executive orders thus far has raised a number of disturbing questions about the adequacy of present procedures for accountability of executive actions. It is clearly an aspect of public administration that requires thorough investigation and perhaps remedial legislation."

Outlook. During the September 28 press conference, reporters queried Church and Mathias on their chances for securing repeal of the national emergency provisions. Church acknowledged that much depended on Congress having the will to pursue its previously relinquished powers. "We live with hope," he stated. "We do have this committee functioning."

He also expressed hope for finding the proper formula for avoiding a presidential veto of any congressional proposals for terminating powers. The cochairman emphasized that there had been close cooperation thus far between the committee and the executive branch. Also, prior to any termination of the four states of national emergency, the Executive would be given a grace period—probably one year—in which it could come to Congress to seek retention of powers thought to be necessary.

Background. As part of its continuing efforts to review executive powers and to reassert congressional authority, the Senate January 6 [1973] approved S. Res 9 to set up a committee to study national emergency legislation.

At the outset of the study it was thought that the state of national emergency dated back to President Truman's December 1950 proclamation of an emergency in response to China's invasion of Korea. However, research by the committee showed that the United States had been living in a state of declared national emergency since March 1933, when Congress ratified President Roosevelt's declaration of an emergency resulting from the Depression.

The discovery pointed up the lack of knowledge in the area of emergency powers. "Because Congress and the public are unaware of the extent of emergency powers, there has never been any notable congressional or public objection made to this state of affairs. Nor have the courts imposed significant limitations," the committee stated in its report.

Committee Hearings

During hearings July 24, three former attorneys general gave their views on emergency powers delegated to the President.

Ramsey Clark told the committee that emergency statutes are an increasing threat to representative government because they do not . . . [respect] the separation of powers. He charged they deny Congress the right to view problems as they emerge. Clark was President Lyndon B. Johnson's acting attorney general in 1966-1967 and attorney general during 1967-1969.

The impact of these statutes depends primarily on the ingenuity of the Executive's legal staff in using them to justify presidential actions, he said.

"A general awareness developed throughout the years (as attorney general) that there were a lot of them (emergency powers) out there and that department lawyers could find one out there to justify anything," Ramsey Clark said.

Attorney general from 1965 to 1966, Nicholas deB. Katzenbach, said, "It is bad constitutional practice, and bad legislative practice, to have such broad delegations on the books without specificity as to the circumstances and occasions on which they can be used." Katzenbach served as deputy attorney general for President John F. Kennedy and attorney general for Johnson until 1966.

Congress. All three of the former attorneys general placed partial blame for the emergency powers on Congress. Tom Clark, attorney general from 1945 to 1949 for President Harry S Truman, said that many times Congress had not taken action with the consequence being attorneys general making decisions without legislative direction.

None argued for the elimination of emergency powers during a national emergency, but all stressed the need for termination of the authority when the specific episode had passed. However, the constitutional authority of some emergency legislation was questioned.

Katzenbach pointed out that differences of interpretation may make some executive actions appear constitutional to some and unconstitutional to others.

Committee cochairman Frank Church (Democrat, Idaho) charged that thousands of bombing missions over Cambodia would not have been flown without being reported to Congress had emergency powers not been in effect.

Church said the two major problems in Congress reclaiming emergency powers were having enough votes to

override a presidential veto of legislation breaking up the
emergency legislation and in receiving executive direction
on which powers are necessary for execution of the office.

Termination. Church and cochairman Charles McCurdy
Mathias Jr. (Republican, Maryland) asked the three witnesses their views on a congressional mandate terminating
all emergency powers within a specified time period after
the mandate's enactment.

The three expressed general approval of the suggested
plan of action, but encouraged thorough investigation of
all emergency legislation before premature use of the proposal to repeal the laws.

THE SECRET WAR [3]

Watergate, the economy, and his health weren't President Nixon's only concerns last week [mid-July of 1973].
He also was harassed and embarrassed by Indochina, the
ramifications of which, like the Biblical poor, promised to
be with us always.

One of the many by-products of the Vietnam war is its
dramatic demonstration of how easy it is for a US President
to wage war by executive action even though the Congress
has made no formal declaration. He can do it openly, as
Harry Truman did in Korea and Lyndon Johnson and
Nixon did in Vietnam, or in secret if necessary.

With the obvious intent of preventing future Vietnam-
style wars, both houses of Congress ignored Nixon's veto
threat and passed bills sharply limiting presidential powers
to wage undeclared war without congressional approval.
And the B-52 bombing in Cambodia continued to embar-
rass the Administration; a former Air Force officer testified
before Congress that official records of at least 3,500 raids
in 1969 and 1970 were falsified to prevent the attacks from
being made public.

[3] "New Moves to Curb War Powers," article by James R. Dickenson. *National Observer.* p 2. Jl. 28, '73. Reprinted with permission from *The National
Observer,* copyright Dow Jones & Company, Inc. 1973.

Nixon's Telegram

The House of Representatives, long supportive of Presidents prosecuting the Indochina war, continued its revolt by passing a bill that would force the Chief Executive in the future to withdraw combat troops within 120 days after they are committed unless he gets congressional approval or a declaration of war. The bill also empowered the Congress to halt the war action itself at any time during the 120 days if both houses pass a concurrent resolution, which the President could not veto.

The House passed the bill, 244 to 170, despite a telegram in which Nixon stated that he "must veto any bill containing the dangerous and unconstitutional restrictions" that he says this bill contains.

The Senate then passed a more stringent bill limiting such troop commitments without congressional sanction to thirty days unless the Congress is unable to meet because of an attack on the United States. The vote was 71 to 18 and the bill was identical to an act that the Senate passed by a 68-to-16 vote last year only to die in conference when the House refused to accept it.

The Senate bill also listed the circumstances under which a President could commit combat troops. These include ordering the armed forces "to repel an armed attack upon the United States, its territories and possessions," to take retaliatory action in event of an attack, and "to forestall the direct and imminent threat of such an attack."

The House bill last week, however, was a clear sign that the two houses can work out some compromise this year. The problem is that there is little likelihood that the House, unlike the Senate, will be able to muster the necessary two-thirds vote to override Nixon's veto; the vote passing the House measure was 32 short of a two-thirds majority.

A Way Out

The President might accept alternative legislation, however. Minority Leader Gerald Ford indicated his belief that Nixon would consider an alternative bill that put a ninety-day limit on troop commitments as long as it didn't give Congress the power to force troop withdrawals through a joint resolution.

The confrontation over war powers was the second in the past two months. In June Congress threatened to cut off appropriations for the bombing in Cambodia, but a compromise was reached on that dispute when Nixon agreed to halt the bombing on August 15.

The bombing in Cambodia has been a problem for Nixon almost from the beginning of his presidency. In May 1969 the story of B-52 raids in Cambodia was leaked to the New York *Times*, acutely embarrassing the President because he had promised secrecy to Prince Norodom Sihanouk, then Cambodia's head of state. Nixon and Sihanouk at that time were in the midst of delicate negotiations to restore diplomatic relations between the two countries, which had been broken in 1965. This leak prompted the Administration to tap the telephones of several newspaper reporters and members of Henry Kissinger's staff; revelation of those taps has added to Nixon's Watergate embarrassment.

Last week Hal S. Knight, a former Air Force major, told the Senate Armed Services Committee that his superiors had ordered him to falsify some records and burn others in 1969 and 1970 to conceal the bombing in Cambodia.

The alterations made it appear that the bombing had been inside South Vietnam rather than Cambodia. Melvin Laird, a top Nixon White House adviser and former Secretary of Defense, said he authorized the Cambodian raids "to protect American life as we began the withdrawal from South Vietnam" but denied ordering the falsification. So did Dr. Kissinger.

Some Confusion

There was some confusion as to who ordered the falsification. Pentagon spokesman Jerry Friedheim at first blamed the Strategic Air Command, but later indicated that the responsibility may lie with the joint military staff that serves the Joint Chiefs of Staff in the Pentagon. [The] Defense spokesman also indicated that the decision to withhold information of the secret bombing from the Armed Services Committee at hearings last spring [1973] may have been made by Deputy Secretary of Defense William P. Clements and Admiral Thomas H. Moorer, chairman of the Joint Chiefs of Staff.

The reasons were familiar. "Diplomatic considerations," Friedheim said. He apparently referred to recent talks that Cambodian President Lon Nol might step down and that the United States is negotiating with—once again—Prince Norodom Sihanouk, who is now in exile in Peking and waiting his chance to return to power in Phnom Penh.

NEW CURBS ON WAR [4]

Congress dealt President Nixon his biggest legislative defeat of the year . . . [on November 7, 1973], as it forced the war-power bill into law over his veto.

The bill limiting the President's power to wage undeclared war swept through the Senate, 75 to 18, after the House had voted 284 to 135 to override the veto. It was the first time in nine tries this year that Congress had mustered the two-thirds vote required to override a veto. And it was the most important issue since it dealt not with dollars but with matters of war and peace.

The Senate vote, as expected, was a comfortable thirteen votes more than needed. The House vote was only four more than required, but for the first time this year House supporters of legislation gained rather than lost strength after a veto.

The law is the culmination of a three-year effort by Congress to prevent the nation from slipping into another Vietnam-type war. Supporters said it is the first time in history

[4] From "Congress Overrides Veto, Enacts War Curbs," article by Richard L. Lyons. Washington *Post*. p 1. N. 8, '73. © The Washington *Post*. Reprinted by permission.

that Congress has enacted a law spelling out the war powers of President and Congress.

The White House issued a statement saying that the President "feels the action seriously undermines this nation's ability to act decisively and convincingly at times of international crisis."

Some members said the House vote reflected the President's low standing because of Watergate. But most voiced the view expressed by Representative John B. Anderson (Republican, Illinois) that "the President wasn't the issue. The powers of Congress was the issue."

The deciding factor in the House vote was the switch of six liberal Democrats from opposition to support of the bill. They had felt that instead of limiting the President's power, the bill recognized presidential powers which they denied existed. But when it came to supporting or opposing the President whose Vietnam war policies they had vigorously opposed, they voted to override.

In the Senate, twenty-five Republicans defected from the Administration position, as did eighty-six House Republicans.

The bill provides that when the President commits US troops to hostilities abroad or "substantially" enlarges the number of US troops equipped for combat in a foreign nation, he must report to Congress within forty-eight hours the circumstances, authority and scope of the action.

The key provisions state that the President must stop the operation after 60 days unless Congress approves his action, though he could continue for 30 more days if necessary to protect US forces. It also provides that Congress can order the operation halted within that period by passing a concurrent resolution that would not be submitted to the President for possible veto.

Mr. Nixon, in his October 24 veto message, said these two provisions intruded on his constitutional powers as Commander in Chief. He challenged the constitutionality of the concurrent resolution approach. And he said actions he took during the recent Mideast crisis "would have been seriously impaired" had the bill then been law.

Congressional supporters of the bill, including Senator John C. Stennis (Democrat, Mississippi), denied that the bill would have prevented or even required the reporting to Congress of actions taken by Mr. Nixon during the Mideast crisis—such as putting US armed forces on alert or sending military aid to Israel.

Senator John Tower (Republican, Texas), who supported the President, said he hoped there would be a quick court test of the constitutionality of the new law.

Supporters of the legislation contend that while a concurrent resolution usually has no legal force, the provision in this law can give validity to such a resolution . . . in the future. They also contend that the legislation overall is a legal and desirable effort by Congress to regain war powers given it by the Constitution. Under the Constitution only Congress can declare war, but Presidents took the nation to war in Korea and Indochina without a declaration. The only congressional support was to appropriate funds for the fighting and adopt the Tonkin Gulf resolution for Vietnam.

Opposition to the bill by the small group of antiwar Democrats was explained during Senate debate by Thomas F. Eagleton (Democrat, Missouri).

Instead of limiting the President's powers, said Eagleton, "this says the President can send us to war anywhere anytime he pleases" for up to ninety days. "We're giving him more power than he ever dreamt he had."

But Senator Jacob K. Javits (Republican, New York), an original sponsor of the legislation, retorted that President Nixon obviously didn't share these views because his veto message said the measure would take away his powers.

Tower, who voted like Eagleton but for opposite reasons, said the measure would restrict a President's power to act in an emergency.

"I realize this is a time when everyone can with impunity kick the President," said Tower. "He's at a low ebb."

Republican Gerald R. Ford (Michigan), House minority leader and Vice President-designate, said the measure contains "potential for disaster." He said it could hurt the President's "credibility" in trying to work with Arabs, Israelis and the Soviet Union to achieve peace in the Mideast.

But Senator Hubert H. Humphrey (Democrat, Minnesota), former Vice President, argued the opposite position: "This is a signal to the world that the President and Congress will work together on matters of national security."

House Majority Leader Thomas P. O'Neill (Democrat, Massachusetts) said nothing in the measure would have prevented Mr. Nixon from acting as he did in the Mideast crisis two weeks ago.

"If the President can deal with the Arabs, Israelis and the Soviet Union, he ought to be willing to deal with the Congress of the United States," said O'Neill.

Representative E. G. Shuster (Republican, Pennsylvania), a freshman and usual supporter of the President, voted to override, saying that when the nation goes to war, "it's the people who fight and die and their fate should be decided by representatives of the people."

Representative Louis Wyman (Republican, New Hampshire), conservative and defense-minded, also voted to override, saying: "The people want no more wars without congressional declaration."

Representative Clement Zablocki (Democrat, Wisconsin), principal author of the final version of the bill, said it would "send a message to the White House that we are partners in matters of war and peace."

In the House, 198 Democrats and 86 Republicans voted to override, while 32 Democrats and 103 Republicans voted to uphold the veto. In the Senate, 50 Democrats and 25 Republicans voted to override, while 3 Democrats and 15 Republicans voted to sustain.

The House erupted in cheers and applause when the override tally was completed. In the Senate, members were more decorous, but the public galleries cheered.

A BALANCE REGAINED? [5]

Another test of the nation's ability to reverse the trend toward executive usurpation of constitutional rights and procedures is scheduled for Wednesday [November 7, 1973] when the House is expected to vote on the question of over-riding a presidential veto of the war-powers bill.

In vetoing the war-powers legislation that had received overwhelming support in both houses, Mr. Nixon called the bill "both unconstitutional and dangerous," adding that it posed "a serious challenge to the wisdom of the Founding Fathers." On the contrary, it is the President who has challenged the essential role the Founding Fathers assigned to Congress in war-making decisions.

It is the Nixon doctrine of unlimited presidential authority to initiate military actions overseas that poses the real threat to American institutions. In a nuclear age it is more important than ever that no man should be granted sole responsibility for steps which, as Secretary Kissinger emphasized during the Middle East crisis, could lead to "unparalleled catastrophe."

The war-powers bill represents a careful, conscientious effort by members of both parties in both houses of Congress, after three years of study and debate, to restore the constitutional system of checks and balances to the war-making process. The bill does not limit the President's valid prerogatives—indeed, it may grant him greater freedom than the Founding Fathers intended to act in emergencies they could not have foreseen.

Nevertheless, by requiring the President to report promptly to Congress on any emergency action and by mandating affirmative congressional approval for any commitment of forces beyond sixty days, the bill preserves the evident intent of the Constitution. It reasserts an essential restraint on presidential authority that has been dangerously dissipated.

[5] Editorial. New York *Times*. p 46. N. 8, '73. © 1973 by The New York Times Company. Reprinted by permission.

A House vote to override the Nixon veto would provide a welcome sign that the Congress, like the Sirica court, is determined to preserve its independence and authority. It would help to restore the country's shaken faith in the integrity of the constitutional processes. [As noted in the previous article, the veto was overriden.—Ed.]

V. EXECUTIVE PRIVILEGE AND IMPOUNDMENT

EDITOR'S INTRODUCTION

Unlike the war-powers issue, the other two constitutional questions—impoundment of funds and executive privilege—were not resolved so clearly. That may be because (at least partially) both are issues the Supreme Court may have to rule on some day. And the Court seems reluctant to involve itself in the power struggle between the other two branches.

The first article in this section is a news analysis that traces how Watergate raised the issue of executive privilege in the first place. The short item that follows is President Richard Nixon's view of executive privilege. The next article reports former Attorney General Richard G. Kleindienst's arguments in support of the President's position.

The fourth item is a historical survey by Arthur Schlesinger, Jr., who looks at executive privilege in the broad sense—that is, whether the President has the right to refuse to testify or submit any of his private papers or tapes to anyone's perusal—including that of Congress.

The fifth article summarizes Senate action that attacks the President's view, arguing that there are only very narrow grounds for the President to refuse to supply information to Congress. Which side is right, of course, is the issue that may eventually be handed over to the Supreme Court to decide.

The last three articles in the section deal with impoundment of funds, one of the more novel problems of our modern society. The President is charged, by law, with keeping employment high and the economy as a whole on an even keel. One way he does this is by controlling the amount of money the Federal Government (by far the nation's biggest spender) lays out during any given period. Congress, on the other hand, authorizes the spending of money. Because spending means jobs, it is usually to congressmen's advantage to vote moneys for projects. Obviously the two views can clash, and they do. To curb inflation President Nixon sought to hold down Government spending, and so he refused to spend some of the moneys Congress had appropriated for him to spend. In short, he impounded the moneys.

The sixth article in the section reports how an incensed Congress sought to take the President to court for not spending the money it had voted. The seventh item, which appeared some nine months later, shows that the issue was not dealt with; rather, lower courts ruled on specific cases involving impoundment of funds.

The last selection in the section is a news story reporting that President Nixon planned to continue the policy of impoundment when he thought it necessary, but less frequently. And so the constitutional question itself may never reach the Supreme Court for resolution.

POINT OF CONFLICT [1]

Congress and the President had been sparring for months over such weighty matters as control of the public purse and the use of war powers. . . . [In mid-March 1973] they were slugging it out over a little-understood and seemingly mundane issue called executive privilege.

Behind both sparring and slugging hovered a basic constitutional question: Could the Congress, weakened over the years by a steady erosion of authority, again become an effective check on a powerful, highly centralized presidential Government? It was not without irony that the incident which brought the mighty issue to a head was a chapter out of last year's dirty politics—the Watergate caper.

[1] "Executive Privilege; a Basic Power Collision," article by John Herbers, of the New York *Times* Washington Bureau. New York *Times*. p E 2. Mr. 18, '73. © 1973 by The New York Times Company. Reprinted by permission.

The Senate Judiciary committee had reopened the Watergate case in the course of confirmation hearings on L. Patrick Gray 3d, President Nixon's choice to become permanent director of the Federal Bureau of Investigation. Mr. Gray testified that as acting director he sent reports from the FBI's inquiry into the matter to John W. Dean 3d, the President's counsel who had been delegated by Mr. Nixon to see if White House staff members were involved in the espionage.

Democratic Senators, suspicious of it all, got the committee to invite Mr. Dean to testify. Acting under President Nixon's policy, he declined, thus raising the issue of executive privilege—the asserted right of a President to withhold certain information from Congress. Mr. Dean said he would answer written questions from the committee that were directly related to the Gray nomination, but this did not satisfy the senators.

On Thursday [March 15], President Nixon spent more than half of a forty-minute press conference defending his position and reiterating that Mr. Dean would not be permitted to testify, even under threat of congressional subpoena. Suggesting that he was willing to face a test in the Supreme Court on the issue, Mr. Nixon said: "Perhaps this is the time to have the highest court of this land make a definite decision with regard to this matter."

"This matter" has been periodically in dispute since George Washington was President. There is nothing in the Constitution about it. No court of any significance has ruled on it. The only precedents are what Presidents have got away with and what checks Congress has been able to bring to bear. Everyone agrees that the President in the conduct of his office and of foreign and military affairs has to have some freedom from congressional interference. Everyone also agrees that congressional oversight is needed over the execution of the laws by strong Presidents.

The issue has arisen repeatedly in the Nixon Administration because an active and aggressive President has accelerated the trend toward centering the great decisions of Government in the White House.

Partisan politics—the fact that the White House is under Republican control, the Congress under Democratic—contributes to the conflict. But some members of both parties in Congress charge Mr. Nixon has extended the power of executive privilege by making it available to more and more officials—even to those no longer in White House employ.

President Nixon and his supporters contend that he has used privilege with restraint, citing the fact that it has been formally invoked only three times in four years. But formal invocation of the privilege, Mr. Nixon's critics say, is not a reliable indicator. Most contests, they insist, never reach the final stage. Many members of Congress just simply give up after the first round. A Library of Congress study found nine incidents in which President Nixon has used executive privilege, not including the instances conceded by the White House.

The President's apparent ruling out of the appearance of Dwight L. Chapin, the former presidential aide, whose name has been linked with the Watergate case, did nothing to soothe feelings in Congress. Neither did Mr. Dean's refusal to appear.

Although Mr. Nixon said he would "cooperate with the Congress" in supplying requested information, he said he trusted that "responsible members of the United States Senate" would not hold Gray's confirmation "as hostage to a decision on Mr. Dean."

The Senate might well do that. It did so in 1972 with the confirmation of Attorney General Richard G. Kleindienst, holding it up until Mr. Nixon agreed to allow Peter M. Flanigan, an assistant, to give limited testimony in the International Telephone and Telegraph case. But Mr. Nixon said he would never yield on Mr. Dean because as White House lawyer he has a "double privilege—the lawyer-client relationship, as well as the presidential privilege."

Whatever happens to Mr. Gray's confirmation, the larger issue of executive privilege remains. It could come to a head in a number of ways as a select committee digs directly into the Watergate affair later in the year and as other committees move against the presidency on such issues as foreign affairs and government organization.

The Judiciary committee could get the matter before the courts by issuing a subpoena for Mr. Dean. But obtaining a Supreme Court ruling—one that would lay down guidelines for proper use of the privilege—could be difficult. The Court traditionally has been reluctant to rule in disputes between the two other branches of Government and might well dispose of the Dean matter on narrow grounds that would be no settlement at all.

EXECUTIVE PRIVILEGE: NIXON'S VIEW [2]

Requests for congressional appearances by members of the President's personal staff present a different situation [from requests for appearances by Cabinet members] and raise different considerations. Such requests have been relatively infrequent through the years, and in past Administrations they have been routinely declined. I have followed the same tradition in my Administration, and I intend to continue it during the remainder of my term.

Under the doctrine of separation of powers, the manner in which the President personally exercises his assigned executive powers is not subject to questioning by another branch of Government. If the President is not subject to such questioning, it is equally inappropriate that members of his staff be so questioned, for their roles are in effect an extension of the presidency.

This tradition rests on more than constitutional doctrine. It is also a practical necessity. To insure the effective discharge of the executive responsibility, a President must be able to place absolute confidence in the advice and

[2] Excerpts from President Nixon's statement on executive privilege. Text from *National Observer*. p 8. Mr. 24, '73.

assistance offered by the members of his staff. And in the performance of their duties for the President, those staff members must not be inhibited by the possibility that their advice and assistance will ever become a matter of public debate, either during their tenure in Government or at a later date. Otherwise, the candor with which advice is rendered and the quality of such assistance will inevitably be compromised and weakened.

What is at stake, therefore, is not simply a question of confidentiality but the integrity of the decision-making process at the very highest levels of our Government. . . .

A member or former member of the President's personal staff normally shall follow the well-established precedent and decline a request for a formal appearance before a committee of the Congress. At the same time, it will continue to be my policy to provide all necessary and relevant information through informal contacts between my present staff and committees of the Congress in ways which preserve intact the constitutional separation of the branches.

ARGUING THE CASE FOR THE PRESIDENT [3]

Congress does not have power to compel anyone in the executive branch to testify or produce documents if the President forbids it, Attorney General Richard G. Kleindienst asserted April 10 [1973].

The sweeping assertion of the doctrine of executive privilege came in the first day of hearings that was marked by repeated clashes of views between the attorney general and Democratic senators.

Kleindienst suggested that Congress' only recourse against the President was a cutoff of executive branch funds or impeachment. He insisted, however, that President Nixon had been judicious in his application of executive privilege and that "99 per cent" of the time Congress gets the witness or document it asks for.

[3] "Kleindienst Hearings." *Congressional Quarterly Almanac.* 29:777. '73. Reprinted by permission.

Kleindienst testified at joint hearings by two Senate Judiciary subcommittees—Separation of Powers and Administrative Practice and Procedure—and the Government Operations Subcommittee on Intergovernmental Relations.

Senator Edmund S. Muskie (Democrat, Maine), chairman of the Intergovernmental Relations subcommittee, had several sharp exchanges with the witness. At one point Muskie, trying to nail down the limits of executive privilege, asked Kleindienst if under his definition, Congress has no power to command the production of the testimony of anyone in the executive branch under any circumstances. Kleindienst hesitated for a moment, and then replied: "If the President so commands."

Muskie called the attorney general's claim "frightening." No Administration in the history of the country had ever asserted this broad a concept, he declared.

Senator J. W. Fulbright (Democrat, Arkansas), testifying later in the day, said Kleindienst appeared to be daring Congress to do something about executive privilege. "I never heard anyone talk like that before," said Fulbright, chairman of the Senate Foreign Relations committee.

Kleindienst made one concession on the President's application of the doctrine, saying criminal matters, like the Watergate investigation, were "uniquely the province of the judiciary." The White House "has stated that even the President's close personal aides will respond to a grand jury inquiry," Kleindienst said. "For crime there can be no haven."

Kleindienst told the senators that the only real limits on executive privilege in a confrontation with Congress were public opinion and the next election. But he suggested another remedy if Congress did not like what the President was doing—impeachment.

"If it feels he is exercising power like a monarch, you could conduct an impeachment proceeding," he said.

The attorney general also repudiated the testimony of Deputy Assistant Attorney General Mary C. Lawton April

4 before the House Foreign Operations and Government Information subcommittee. At that hearing, Lawton, of the office of legal counsel, said executive privilege did not apply to White House aides if the purpose was to prevent congressional investigations of criminal activity.

She told the subcommittee that the privilege would not cover White House counsel John W. Dean 3d if he obstructed justice in the FBI's investigation of the Watergate affair.

Kleindienst said he disagreed with Lawton's testimony.

Clark M. Clifford, former secretary of defense and White House aide to President Truman, said the President could legitimately exercise executive privilege in his role as Commander in Chief and as Chief Executive. But his other role, that of a political party leader, should be open to congressional investigation, Clifford said.

This was in reference to the Watergate affair, for which "the time has come for a showdown," Clifford stated. He said Watergate presented a clear political issue and proposed that witnesses who refused to appear be cited for contempt and their cases turned over to the courts.

A House Republican leader told the joint hearing April 11 he wanted to stress "in the strongest possible terms my utter shock and dismay" at Kleindienst's testimony. John B. Anderson of Illinois, chairman of the House Republican Conference, said the attorney general's description of the extent of the power represented a "truly alarming expansion."

Kleindienst "has thrown down the gauntlet," he said. "If this Congress is to preserve even a semblance of integrity and independence it must act immediately to nullify the sweeping claim" of the attorney general.

Senator Adlai E. Stevenson III testified that the only way to curb executive branch use of the privilege was for Congress to pass a bill defining and limiting it.

Nixon and Kleindienst were "torturing the doctrine of separation of powers into a doctrine of uncontrolled power for one branch of government," Stevenson declared.

HISTORICAL PRECEDENTS [4]

President Nixon has committed himself to the proposition that his "constitutional obligation to preserve intact the powers and prerogatives of the presidency" compels him to refuse the Ervin committee both his own testimony and access to his White House papers and tapes. In making this refusal, the President evidently supposes that he is doing no more than defend the Constitution and the separation of powers in the manner of all his predecessors. The question for today's seminar is whether the President's position is historically sound.

It has happened rarely enough in our history that a court or a committee of Congress has called for a President's testimony. In consequence our history is not exactly rich in precedent on the question whether the separation of powers protects the presidency from compulsory process by the other branches of government. None the less, a few episodes do bear rather directly on President Nixon's argument.

The most celebrated case goes back to 1807 when Chief Justice John Marshall, sitting in circuit as judge in the trial at Richmond, Virginia, of Aaron Burr for treason, subpoenaed President Jefferson. In doing so, Marshall began by denying that it was "incompatible" with presidential dignity for Jefferson to submit to the process of the court. The English principle that the king could do no wrong, Marshall said, did not apply to the United States, where the President could be impeached and removed from office. "That the President of the United States may be subpoenaed, and examined as a witness, and required to produce any paper in his possession," Marshall said in the course of the trial, "is not controverted."

Having laid down the general principle, Marshall, a realistic judge, was not prepared to force it to the point of

[4] "The Presidency and the Law," article by Arthur Schlesinger, Jr., Albert Schweitzer Professor of the Humanities at the City University of New York and winner of Pulitzer prizes in history and biography. *Wall Street Journal.* p 10. Jl. 19, '73. Reprinted by permission of the author.

showdown. So the subpoena stipulated that the transmission to the court of specified documents "will be admitted as sufficient observance of the process, without the personal attendance . . . of the person therein named." As for Jefferson, he could hardly contest the general principle without coming close to saying that the President could do no wrong. But he was damned if he would go to Richmond, which of course, Marshall had cannily not asked him to do. What he did was to send the documents requested and to offer testimony by deposition. At the same time, he sketched out, mostly in private letters, a theory about Presidents and subpoenas.

While conceding that "all persons owe obedience to subpoenas," Jefferson contended that a President had a still higher obligation to the "particular set of duties imposed on him." His theory, in short, was not that the President was *per se* immune to subpoena, but that the courts could not expect to command "the Executive to abandon superior duties" at will. If a President were obliged to honor every subpoena, the courts could breach the separation of powers, keep the President "constantly trudging from north and south and east and west, and withdraw him entirely from his constitutional duties."

An Agreeable Compromise

The matter thus ended with Marshall asserting a constitutional right to subpoena Presidents and Jefferson standing on a practical right not to show up in court. Marshall, in other words, said that the President was subject to the same law as every other American citizen, and Jefferson said: Well, yes, but the President also had more solemn responsibilities than any other American citizen, and this must be taken into account. Both Marshall and Jefferson were surely correct. Their collective response suggests that the answer in such cases lies in striking a balance between the President's obligation to his official duties, on the one

hand, and the importance of a particular case and the in-
dispensability of the President's testimony on the other.

Sixty years after this incident the state of Mississippi
tried to enjoin President Andrew Johnson from enforcing
the Reconstruction statutes. The case went to the Supreme
Court, which declared the President immune to judicial
jurisdiction in matters arising from the performance of his
official duties. But the decision in *Mississippi v. Johnson* did
not convey total presidential exemption from judicial or
legislative process. Carrying out the law is an official duty;
breaking it, for example, is not. As the attorney general who
argued Johnson's case put it to the Court, he was not rely-
ing "upon any personal immunity that the individual has
who happens to be President; upon any idea that he cannot
do wrong; upon any idea that there is any particular sanc-
tity belonging to him as an individual, as is the case with
one who has royal blood in his veins." (Nor, for that matter,
did the decision mean that Presidents were never to appear
in court. Johnson's successor, President Grant, wanted to
testify as a witness for the defense when his private secretary was prosecuted by his own Department of Justice and
did file a deposition on the unfortunate General Babcock's
behalf.)

In June 1972 the Supreme Court reinforced Marshall's
position of 1807. In a decision made possible by the united
vote of President Nixon's own appointments, the Court emphatically reaffirmed the old principle that "the public has
a right to *every man's* evidence" (emphasis added). This was
in the case of *Branzburg v. Hayes*, better known in the trade
as the Caldwell case, where newspapermen were ordered to
disclose their sources to grand juries. To underline its point,
the Court quoted Jeremy Bentham: "Were the Prince of
Wales, the Archbishop of Canterbury, and the Lord High
Chancellor to be passing by in the same coach while a
chimney-sweeper and a barrow-woman were in dispute about
a half-pennyworth of apples, and the chimney-sweeper or
the barrow-woman were to think it proper to call upon them

for their evidence, could they refuse it? No, most certainly."
This rule, handed down by President Nixon's own Justices,
is tougher than Jefferson's persuasive claim that, in the case
at least of the President, the superior call of official duties
might well make it impossible for him to testify about a
half-pennyworth of apples.

These cases involved the right of courts to command the
appearance of citizens, including Presidents. At this stage,
President Nixon faces only the separate but related issue of
congressional committees. Now the separation of powers has
never been conceived as inhibiting all direct intercourse
between Presidents and Congress. Washington himself on a
famous occasion in 1789 went to Congress to ask its advice
on a treaty. It was Congress, and not the President, that
thought this a poor idea and discouraged Washington from
trying it again. Lincoln appeared before the House Judiciary committee in 1862 to discuss the leak of his State of the
Union Message to the New York *Herald* and is supposed
also to have gone to a session of the Committee on the
Conduct of the War to deny that his wife was a Confederate
spy. Numerous Presidents have invited committees of Congress to chat with them on their own turf.

These were all occasions when Presidents wished to appear. But what if a President did not wish to appear? Obviously this was not a situation that Presidents were much
inclined to anticipate. But Andrew Jackson, that stoutest
of all defenders of the presidential prerogative, said that he
was "willing upon all proper occasions to give to either
branch of the Legislature any information in my possession
that can be useful in the execution of the appropriate
duties confided to them." In 1846 James K. Polk, another
notable champion of the presidency, considered the question
in more detail. The House of Representatives had formally
requested him to turn over information about secret intelligence operations conducted by the previous Administration.
Polk declined to do so. At the same time, he conceded that
the House remained, in the phrase hallowed by the English

parliamentary tradition, "the grand inquest of the nation." If its members had any reason to believe there had been "malversation" in office (the Oxford English Dictionary defines "malversation" as "corrupt behaviour in a position of trust"), then, Polk said, "all the archives and papers of the executive department, public or private, would be subject to the inspection and control of a committee of their body and every facility in the power of the Executive be afforded to enable them to prosecute the investigation." Above all, if the House wished to inquire into executive misconduct with a view to the exercise of its power of impeachment, "The power of the House in the pursuit of this object would penetrate into the most secret recesses of the executive departments. *It could command the attendance of any and every agent of the government, and compel them to produce all papers, public or private, official or unofficial, and to testify on oath to all facts within their knowledge*" (emphasis added). As Marshall had said that a grand jury could require the testimony of a President, Polk now said that the House of Representatives in cases of malversation could inspect the papers of a President and, if it were conducting an inquiry with a view to impeachment, could require his personal testimony under oath.

Mr. Nixon's Rejection

President Nixon has plainly rejected the views of Chief Justice Marshall and President Polk. Since Marshall and Polk lived a little closer to the time of the Constitutional Convention, it may be assumed that they had a better idea of what the Founding Fathers intended. Nor is our President on firmer ground when he also rejects the compromise proposal that he or his counsel peruse and identify select documents for release for the Ervin committee. "Such a course, I have concluded, would inevitably result in the attrition, and the eventual destruction, of the indispensable principle of the confidentiality of presidential papers." This is a really footling point. If the President thinks that sacred constitutional principles are involved, he can assert those principles and still open the papers as a voluntary decision, entirely without prejudice to his constitutional rights. As Wilson told Congress when he sent troops to Vera Cruz, "I could do what is necessary . . . without recourse to the Congress and yet not exceed my constitutional powers as President, but I do not wish to act in a matter of so grave consequence except in close conference and cooperation."

Nor is President Nixon's invocation of President Truman's refusal to appear before the House Un-American Activities Committee in 1953 to the point. In that case the subpoena, issued by the forgotten and unlamented Harold Velde, did not even specify the matters on which the committee sought the former President's testimony. This was a pure case of publicity seeking and harassment; and Truman, though his historical recital was inaccurate, turned back the subpoena with justified scorn. But Sam Ervin is no Harold Velde; and the balance of considerations is additionaly different when a President is called upon to discuss malversation on the part of his own White House staff.

The theory of the separation of powers currently espoused by President Nixon is far more rigid than that held by the Founding Fathers. All that the separation of powers meant, Madison wrote in the forty-eighth *Federalist*, was "that the powers belonging to one of the departments ought not to be directly and completely administered by either of the other departments." The President could not legislate, nor the Congress execute the law, and neither could render judicial decisions. But the Constitution did not erect a wall of separation between Congress and the presidency. As Madison put it, unless the coordinate branches "be so far connected and blended as to give to each a constitutional control over the others, the degree of separation which the maxim requires, as essential to a free government, can never in practice be duly maintained."

A Relative Argument

This does not mean that President Nixon would not be right to defend the presidency from casual and random demands whether congressional or judicial. But the argument here is relative, not absolute. It depends on striking a balance between the demands and presidential duties, not on some unconditional injunction of the Constitution. The balance in nearly all past cases has been in favor of the executive branch, which is why no President since Jefferson has been subpoenaed and why no Cabinet member has ever been held in contempt for refusal to honor a subpoena. No sensible court or congressional committee would issue a subpoena unless it had both the most compelling and demonstrable need for presidential testimony and strong support in responsible opinion as well. But this is a very different matter from President Nixon's claim that there is some absolute constitutional principle justifying his unconditional refusal to give testimony to the Ervin committee on a matter of the gravest national consequence in which his personal knowledge and his White House papers are indispensable. Let him read and reflect on President Polk's message to the House of Representatives on April 20, 1846.

SENATE ACTION [5]

The Senate by voice vote December 18 [1973] approved two measures (S 2432, S Con Res 30) setting forth procedures for congressional and judicial enforcement of Congress' right to obtain information from Federal officials.

Delivering "a firm legislative rebuttal" to "recent and increasing assertions of executive privilege to withhold information from Congress and its committees," the Senate endorsed the bill and the resolution which made explicit the authority of Congress to obtain information and the responsibility of Federal officials to provide information when requested.

[5] From "Executive Privilege." *Congressional Quarterly Almanac.* 29:776-7. '73. Reprinted by permission.

Written as an amendment to the Legislative Reorganization Act of 1970, S 2432 made clear that all requested information must be provided unless the President himself in writing instructed that the information be withheld. The bill also provided for procedures by which Congress could move to override a claim of privilege, to subpoena the information and to go to court if the subpoena was not complied with.

S Con Res 30 contained similar stipulations concerning the right of Congress to obtain information and the duty of Federal officials to provide it. The resolution—which if approved by the House would become part of the rules and procedures of Congress, but not a public law—provided for congressional subpoena of information withheld and for proceedings leading to a holding of contempt of Congress for noncompliance with a subpoena. The House did not act on either measure before the end of the session.

Committee Action

"Your power to get what the President knows is in the President's hands," stated then-Attorney General Richard G. Kleindienst April 10 to the congressional subcommittees holding hearings on executive privilege. And that claim of absolute privilege was the central target of S 2432, reported by the Committee on Government Operations December 11 (S Rept 93-612). [See "Arguing the Case for the President," above in this section.]

Lengthy hearings on the problem of obtaining information from an unwilling executive branch had been held by a variety of congressional subcommittees in 1971, 1972 and 1973. Upset by such executive withholding in the foreign affairs field, various members of Congress had tried in 1973 to add language to foreign affairs measures cutting off funds to any foreign policy agency which refused to provide requested information. None of the provisions had survived House-Senate conferences. . . .

If the absolute privilege claimed by Kleindienst did in

fact exist, said the committee report, "the power of the executive branch to screen the conduct of its officials from inquiry would overwhelm and invalidate the power of Congress to make those inquiries." Therefore, legislation was needed, to make clear that "the executive may seek to deny information to the legislative branch; that the legislative branch may seek to compel the production of the information despite a claim of privilege; and that the judiciary, in the event the other two branches fail to resolve their disagreement, should be called upon to decide the outcome."

The bill as reported, stated the committee, was "an essential expression of the principle that the executive lacks the power to determine alone what information shall be made available to the Congress." The report noted that the committee had rejected an amendment proposed by Senator William V. Roth Jr. (Republican, Delaware) which would have set out certain categories of information likely to be found privileged and beyond the reach of Congress. The committee preferred that such determination be made on a case-by-case basis.

Provisions

As passed by the Senate, S 2432 amended the Legislative Reorganization Act of 1970 to:

Write into law the duty of Federal officials and employees to provide Congress and its committees with requested information, unless they are instructed by the President in writing not to do so

Authorize the appropriate committee chairman or leader of the majority or minority in the chamber to issue subpoenas compelling the production of information withheld at presidential instruction

Authorize those same officials, if the subpoena is not complied with, to file civil suits in Federal district court in the District of Columbia for enforcement of the subpoena

Conferred on the Federal District Court for the District of Columbia jurisdiction over such cases (Federal Judge

John J. Sirica dismissed the Senate Watergate committee's case for enforcement of its subpoenas because Congress had not, at that time, acted to grant his court this jurisdiction.)

Authorized the court to enforce the subpoenas by a mandatory injunction or other order to modify the subpoenas or to set them aside

Provided that the Select Committee on Standards and Conduct of the Senate and the House Committee on Standards of Official Conduct should investigate any breach of the confidentiality of information made available to Congress by Federal officials

The provisions of S Con Res 30 were the same, except that the resolution did not contain language authorizing court action, but instead provided for each chamber to move toward citing a person who refused to comply with a subpoena for contempt of Congress.

A QUESTION OF SPENDING [6]

Some of the Senate's most powerful Democratic leaders are challenging in court President Nixon's right to impound funds appropriated by Congress.

This legal move, initiated by Senator Sam J. Ervin (Democrat) of North Carolina, is part of a broad effort to reassert the constitutional right of Congress to control Federal spending.

The impending money struggle between White House and Congress raises legal, political, and social issues, with millions of poor Americans caught in the middle.

Senator Ervin and seventeen other Democratic senators, joined by three congressmen and Ralph Nader's Public Citizen, Inc., chose a Missouri state highway money case as the opening field of battle.

[6] "Courts, Congress Test Nixon Refusal to Spend," article by Harry B. Ellis, business and financial correspondent of *The Christian Science Monitor. Christian Science Monitor.* p 7. Ja. 4, '73. Reprinted by permission from *The Christian Science Monitor.* © 1973 The Christian Science Publishing Society. All rights reserved.

They intervened as friends of the court in a suit brought against the United States Government by the State Highway Commission of Missouri, which is trying to pry loose highway trust funds impounded by Secretary of Transportation John A. Volpe.

Impoundment Challenged

On June 19, 1972, a Federal district judge ruled that the President, through Mr. Volpe, lacked the right to impound, or withhold, these funds, which had been appropriated by Congress.

The judge cited a clause in the Federal-aid highway act excluding impoundment except to prevent unacceptable depletion of funds.

The Government appealed the ruling to the United States Eighth Circuit Court of Appeals in St. Louis, where the case now rests. It is here that the senators intervened.

Their intervention, remarked a senatorial aide, "has no legal effect, but broadens the impact of the case." He predicted that whichever side loses the appeal—the United States Government or the Missouri State Highway Commission—might appeal the ruling to the Supreme Court of the United States for final decision.

But the Missouri highway case, however it comes out, presumably will hinge on the narrow issue of the specific language of Congress in forbidding impoundment of highway trust funds. Since that time President Nixon, determined to hold Federal spending to $250 billion in fiscal year 1973, has impounded "$10 to $12 billion in other funds," according to a Senate staffer.

These funds, for the most part, were not restricted by specific anti-impoundment clauses. So the outcome of the Missouri case will not necessarily affect them.

Recently the President withheld $6 billion of the $11 billion appropriated by Congress to clean up the nation's waterways. New York City now is suing for release of those impounded funds, and other suits may develop.

Mr. Nixon, among other things, also has terminated the Rural Environmental Assistance Program, cut back emergency loans and conservation payments to farmers, and—in the view of the Ervin-led senatorial group—threatens to curtail other social programs.

More than $200 billion of every Federal budget is committed to long-term programs—including interest on the Federal debt, Social Security and other income maintenance policies, and defense—and cannot be trimmed by the President.

Yet he says he must slice still another $7 billion to $10 billion from money appropriated by Congress to bring spending down to $250 billion in this fiscal year. To spend above this level, insists Mr. Nixon, would invite inflation and higher taxes.

Political and Social Aspects

From the nature of cuts already made and of options remaining to the President, liberal lawmakers fear that programs designed to help poor Americans will suffer.

Thus the struggle over money takes on political and social overtones. Senator Ervin, joined by Majority Leader Mike Mansfield (Democrat) of Montana, Majority Whip Robert C. Byrd (Democrat) of West Virginia, and other Democratic senators, is determined to carry the fight to the floor of Congress.

"The power of the purse," declared Senator Ervin, "belongs exclusively to Congress under the Constitution. This effort [in the Missouri court case] by the committee chairmen and the majority leaders forcefully illustrates their belief that Congress must act to recapture the powers that have slipped from it."

The senatorial friends of the court include, in addition to the majority leader and whip, the Democratic chairmen of 14 of the Senate's 17 standing committees.

ADMINSTRATION, DESPITE LOSSES IN COURT, STILL IMPOUNDS FUNDS [7]

The Nixon Administration's impoundment policies, roundly condemned by members of Congress, are taking a nearly unanimous beating in the courts as well. Of thirty cases decided by early September [1973], most at the lower court level, the Government can claim only five victories, according to a study by the Library of Congress.

Typical are suits brought by states and private groups against the Department of Health, Education, and Welfare (HEW) aimed at prying loose some of the $1.8 billion the department impounded for health and education programs in fiscal 1973. Preliminary rulings have required HEW to set aside about $559 million pending final settlement of the cases, according to an HEW budget official.

No Discretion

The rulings, for the most part, have swept aside the Administration's contention that the President can withhold funds to control inflation or prevent a tax increase, if Congress specifically has directed that funds for certain programs be spent.

Ordering HEW to take steps to release $52.1 million in mental health funds August 3, Federal District Court Judge Gerhard A. Gesell ruled that the President "does not have complete discretion to pick and choose between programs when some of them are made mandatory by conscious, deliberate congressional action."

Spending Plan—Whose?

The HEW spending controversy stemmed from the fact that regular appropriations for the department never were enacted for fiscal 1973. Instead, funding was covered by a continuing resolution subject to hotly debated interpretations.

[7] "HEW Impoundments," news release, by Elizabeth Bowman. Copyright 1973 by Congressional Quarterly, Inc. Reprinted by permission.

Congress contends that spending should be governed by funds included in a first fiscal 1973 appropriations bill, vetoed by the President. The Administration rejected this interpretation, basing its self-imposed "spending plan" on what the President had proposed for the programs in fiscal 1973.

Representative Daniel J. Flood (Democrat, Pennsylvania), chairman of the House subcommittee on HEW appropriations, complained the spending plan was about as fixed as a "railroad timetable." But by the close of the fiscal year June 30, HEW by its own admission had impounded $1.1 billion for health programs and more than $600 million for education programs—under the congressionally recognized spending plan, that is.

Spending Requirement

While Government attorneys have stressed the President's general authority to impound funds, those challenging the impoundments have based their arguments on special provisions of two 1970 acts requiring funds appropriated for most health and education programs to be available for expenditure until the end of a fiscal year. Cutting off program funds before June 30, 1973, violated the clear congressional intent of these provisions, they argued.

HEW Secretary Caspar W. Weinberger termed the special provisions "unclear and most debatable" in June, although some senators contend that he agreed in January that they required spending. Weinberger claimed it would be "absurd" for HEW to base spending on levels vetoed by the President under the congressional interpretation of the continuing resolution.

Representative Paul G. Rogers (Democrat, Florida), chairman of the House health subcommittee, found it equally "ludicrous that people who are supposed to receive health funds have to go to court to get the secretary of HEW to carry out the laws that the Congress passed." Rogers has threatened to hold hearings to seek resignations of HEW officials "who failed to carry out the law."

Weinberger has pledged to appeal all adverse rulings up to the Supreme Court if necessary, although the Government did not appeal other unfavorable rulings in impoundment cases dealing with programs outside HEW. Pending appeal, Weinberger claims HEW can ignore lower court rulings.

A Georgia suit challenging impoundment of highway, water pollution and education funds could reach the Supreme Court during its 1973–74 term if the court agrees to hear the case directly without lower court action. The Justice department, fighting dozens of impoundment suits, is thought sympathetic to an early decision by the Supreme Court.

In the meantime, HEW has continued its impoundment pattern into fiscal 1974. Without a Supreme Court decision or final action by Congress on new HEW appropriations or general anti-impoundment legislation, some groups are readying new court challenges to fiscal 1974 impoundments.

PARTING SHOT [8]

President Nixon will continue trying to cut public spending by impounding funds appropriated by Congress, but hopes to do less of it . . . [in 1974], a White House official told the Associated Press. . . . Impoundments by the President have been a source of friction with Congress . . . [in 1973].

Frederic V. Malek, deputy director of the Office of Management and Budget, said the President's decision . . . to release $1.1 billion in impounded health and education funds does not indicate a change in Mr. Nixon's view that he has the constitutional right to withhold congressionally appropriated funds.

[8] From "Nixon to Continue Impounding Funds." *Christian Science Monitor.* p 8. D. 21, '73. Reprinted by permission from *The Christian Science Monitor.* © 1973 The Christian Science Publishing Society. All rights reserved.

Mr. Malek said the White House had released health and education funds because it has consistently lost suits challenging impoundment in the courts. But he noted the Administration still hopes to win court challenges in impoundments not involving health and education funds.

VI. IMPEACHMENT STEPS BEGIN

EDITOR'S INTRODUCTION

The disputes over constitutional questions, along with the revelations of Watergate, led right back to the Constitution. In this instance they led, however, to the provisions for bringing charges against the President. In short, the process of impeachment had been set in motion. This section deals with the legal and mechanical preludes to impeachment. It also deals with some of the constitutional questions that continue to be raised.

The first item in the section is a tabulation enumerating the constitutional basis for impeachment and a list of some of the constitutional powers the President has at his disposal to defend himself.

The next selection, a question-and-answer article, deals with the basic questions of impeachment. Who must do what, when, and to whom? But it also points out that the grounds for impeachment—the language that defines impeachment—are very vague. It is a critical vagueness because it means that someone must interpret the specifics. And each side in the issue, of course, has a differing view.

One vague area is discussed at length in the article that follows. Must the President have committed a criminal offense in order to be impeached? Or does the Constitution's phrase "high crimes and misdemeanors" mean that the President can be impeached for, say, dereliction of duty or mismanagement in office?

The next article raises yet another key issue. Is a President responsible for the acts, or misdeeds, of those who work for him? The Constitution fails to spell out his responsibility. Yet the question is of critical importance, because, as the article states, White House aides have been cited on criminal charges by at least one grand jury. Does it follow that the President is guilty as well? There are arguments for both sides.

The power of subpoena is more important than it may at first seem. It means that the Judiciary committee has the power of the full House of Representatives behind it when it asks for evidence either in the form of tapes or through witnesses. To ignore one of its subpoenas means risking the grave charge of contempt of Congress.

Strong as the congressional hand may seem, the President is not without some powers of his own. The strongest of these is, in effect, to bypass the Congress by taking his case to the people. This is precisely what President Nixon sought to do. Each time, of course, the aim was to make his position seem fair and reasonable. Repeatedly, the President went on nationwide television to explain his side. And, repeatedly, some new development worsened his position. In early May 1974 the President made his boldest bid for public sympathy: the release of voluminous edited transcripts of taped White House discussions of Watergate. The last selection here details that gamble. It also notes that the House Judiciary committee had begun its hearings on impeachment.

Thus the stage for the great showdown between Congress and the Executive was set.

THE CONSTITUTION ON IMPEACHMENT [1]

Article I, Section 2

The House of Representatives . . . shall have the sole Power of Impeachment.

Article I, Section 3

The Senate shall have the sole Power to try all Impeachments. When sitting for that Purpose, they shall be on Oath

[1] Text from "Presidential Impeachment," report by Mary Costello, staff writer. *Editorial Research Reports.* v 2, no 21:934. D. 5, '73. Reprinted by permission.

of Affirmation. When the President of the United States is tried, the Chief Justice shall preside: And no Person shall be convicted without the Concurrence of two thirds of the Members present.

Judgment in Cases of Impeachment shall not extend further than to removal from Office and disqualification to hold and enjoy any Office of Honor, Trust or Profit under the United States: but the Party convicted shall nevertheless be liable and subject to Indictment, Trial, Judgment and Punishment, according to Law.

Article II, Section 2

The President shall have Power to grant Reprieves and Pardons for Offenses against the United States, except in Cases of Impeachment.

Article II, Section 4

The President, Vice President and all civil Officers of the United States shall be removed from Office on Impeachment for, and Conviction of, Treason, Bribery, or other high Crimes and Misdemeanors.

Article III, Section 2

The Trial of all Crimes, except in Cases of Impeachment, shall be by jury.

THE MECHANICS OF IMPEACHMENT [2]

Reprinted from *U.S. News & World Report.*

What, exactly, is impeachment? Impeachment is the first of two constitutional steps in removing a President or other high Federal official in the executive or judiciary branches. Impeachment is the way the United States House of Representatives accuses or charges an official.

Is impeachment the same as removing a person from office? No. Many people use the term *impeachment* loosely

[2] "Answers to Questions on Impeachment." *U.S. News & World Report.* 76:29-30. Ap. 8, '74.

to mean the removal of an official. That is a mistaken use of the word. Impeachment is somewhat similar to an indictment brought by a grand jury—that is, it is an accusation, not a conviction.

Then how is a President or an official actually removed from office? That can be done by the Senate after the House impeaches. In brief, the House charges and acts as prosecutor. The Senate chamber becomes a kind of courtroom. The Senate holds a trial, and members of the Senate act as jury.

Does each house of Congress act by a simple majority vote? Impeachment by the House of Representative requires a simple majority of those members present. Conviction by the Senate, however, requires a two-thirds vote of the members present.

What are the grounds for impeachment? Article II, Section 4 of the Constitution states: "The President, Vice President and all civil officers of the United States shall be removed from office on impeachment for, and conviction of, treason, bribery or other high crimes and misdemeanors."

Is there some controversy over what impeachable "high crimes and misdemeanors" are? Yes. There is very little dispute over the meaning of treason or bribery. But the history of impeachments is marked by lengthy arguments over how to define "high crimes and misdemeanors." They are not spelled out in the Constitution.

Do the debates of the Constitutional Convention provide any clues? In the Constitutional Convention of 1787, discussion of impeachable offenses included "malpractice or neglect of duty," "treason, bribery or corruption," "treason or bribery" alone and "maladministration." Finally, the phrase "treason, bribery or other high crimes and misdemeanors" was settled upon.

Impeachment, then, turns mainly on how the phrase "high crimes and misdemeanors" is interpreted? That is correct. Recently the Justice department summed it up this way: "There are persuasive grounds for arguing both the narrow view that a violation of criminal law is required and the broader view that certain noncriminal 'political offenses' may justify impeachment."

What view does the White House take? President Nixon last February [1974] said: "It is the opinion of the White House counsel and a number of constitutional lawyers . . . that a criminal offense on the part of the President is the requirement for impeachment."

White House lawyers put it this way: "Impeachment of a President should be resorted to only for cases of the gravest kind—the commission of a crime named in the Constitution or a criminal offense against the laws of the United States. . . . A President may only be impeached for indictable crimes."

Is a broader view taken in Congress? In some quarters. For instance, the bipartisan staff of the House Judiciary committee, which has been studying impeachment, has stated: "The American experience with impeachment reflects the principle that impeachable conduct need not be criminal. . . . Some of the most grievous offenses against our constitutional form of government may not entail violations of the criminal law. . . . In the English practice and in several of the American impeachments, the criminality issue was not raised at all. The emphasis has been on the significant effects of the conduct: undermining the integrity of the office, disregard of the constitutional duties and oath of office, arrogation of power, abuse of the governmental process, adverse impact on the system of government. Clearly, these effects can be brought about in ways not anticipated by the criminal law."

Can a President be impeached for the conduct of the men under him? James Madison, one of the framers of the Constitution, said: "I think it is absolutely necessary that the President should have the power of removing [his assistants] from office; it will make him, in a peculiar manner, responsible for their conduct and subject him to impeachment himself, if he suffers them to perpetrate with impunity high crimes and misdemeanors against the United States or neglects to superintend their conduct, so as to check their excesses."

However, this question has never been formally decided.

How often has the impeachment process been used? Not very often. It is a long and often painful process.

One President, Andrew Johnson, and one Justice of the Supreme Court, Samuel Chase, were impeached. Neither, however, was convicted. Action was initiated against two other Presidents in addition to Mr. Nixon—John Tyler and Herbert Hoover—but the House refused to impeach them.

In all, only 13 impeachments have been voted by the House, and only 11 of these went to trial before the Senate. Four defendants, each a Federal judge, were convicted.

What happened in the impeachment of Andrew Johnson? He was accused of "high crimes and misdemeanors" rooted in post-Civil War animosities. Mr. Johnson was under fire from "radical Reconstructionists" in Congress because of his conciliatory attitude toward the defeated South. When he fired Secretary of War Edwin M. Stanton in 1868, he was accused of violating the Tenure of Office Act. This Act gave the Senate the right to decide whom the President could remove from his Cabinet. He was also accused of making anti-Congress speeches.

What was the vote? The House impeached Mr. Johnson by a vote of 128 to 47. But the vote in the Senate was 35 for conviction and 19 for acquittal—just one vote short of the two-thirds majority necessary for conviction.

Impeachment in the House

How is impeachment action started? In the case of a President, one or more members of the House introduces an impeachment resolution.

The Speaker of the House then has three options: He may: (1) rule the resolution, in effect, out of order; (2) refer the resolution, by vote of the House, to a committee to investigate; or, (3) put the resolution directly to a vote, something that has never happened.

If the House wishes to proceed, what does it usually do? It votes for a committee to investigate the preliminary charges—as it did in the case of President Nixon. In this century that committee has been the Judiciary committee, which is composed of 21 Democrats and 17 Republicans at present.

Does the Federal official under investigation have the right to have counsel present during the committee's investigation? That is a matter now under dispute. In some of the nation's impeachment cases, including the case of Andrew Johnson, the official under investigation did not have counsel present during preliminary House proceedings. In others, though, defense lawyers were permitted to play a role in such proceedings. It is up to the House Judiciary committee to decide: [President Richard Nixon's attorney won the right to participate in the committee's investigation and interrogation.—Ed.]

Does the Judiciary committee have to vote one way or the other on impeachment? Yes, it must report to the full House either a resolution of impeachment or a recommendation against impeachment. A resolution in favor of impeachment includes articles of impeachment, each detailing a specific charge.

Those members of the committee who are in the minority have the right to issue a minority report—appearing at the same time as the majority report—setting forth the arguments against impeachment.

Suppose the Judiciary committee recommends against impeachment. Does that end the matter? Not necessarily. The House can still impeach by majority vote.

If the committee recommends impeachment what is the next step? The impeachment resolution is "privileged"— that is, it goes straight to the House floor. It does not need approval of the Rules committee, as regular legislation does.

Are there limits on debate in the House? Under present practice, the House votes a total time limit on debate. As a rule each member is allowed no more than one hour's time to speak during the debate. The House leadership controls the time. Most speakers in the past have talked much less than the one hour allowed.

Is the President represented during the House debate? Not according to precedent. Neither he nor an agent of the White House appears.

Does the House vote on each separate charge in the articles of impeachment? No, the House votes on the impeachment resolution as a whole, according to recent precedent. If the resolution is adopted, the House then picks "managers" to direct the prosecution in the Senate trial.

How are these managers picked? In one of two ways: The House can adopt a resolution allowing the Speaker of the House to name the managers. Or the Speaker can name managers and then present them in resolutions to be passed by the House. In the latter case, each manager must be approved, by majority vote, in separate resolutions.

In recent times, managers have usually been members of the Judiciary committee and, since they are picked to carry out the will of the House, are on the side opposed to the President or other official impeached. The managers, usually numbering from three to seven, may include members of both parties.

Trial in the Senate

The Senate takes over at that point? Yes. In the case of a President, the Senate informs the Chief Justice of the United States, who will be the presiding officer, that the articles of impeachment have been received. The Senate also orders a summons served on the President, reciting the articles of impeachment and asking for an answer to the charges. The summons also notifies the President to appear at his trial in person or to be represented by an attorney.

The President is permitted to attend the trial, then? Yes, if he wishes. He also has the right to appear as a witness, but in that case he would be subject to cross-examination under oath. Andrew Johnson did not appear on the floor during his trial.

How long after the House votes to impeach does the Senate trial start? No requirement is fixed by law. In the case of President Johnson, the Senate trial began five weeks after the House vote.

Suppose the House this year impeached the President, but the Senate could not act until next year, when another Congress would have been seated. Must the House start proceedings over again? The House would have to pick managers again. But the Senate could try the President next year without any other action by the House. If the House does not vote on impeachment this year [1974], however, then it must start its proceedings all over again if it wants to go ahead with impeachment in 1975 or 1976.

How is the Senate trial conducted? On the date set, the Senate opens the trial at noon in the Senate chamber. The Chief Justice is sworn and then administers an oath to the Senators, swearing them to do "impartial justice." Rules of evidence, substantially similar to those used in courts, will be interpreted by the Chief Justice. His rulings, however, can be overturned by a Senate vote.

Day by day, except on Sundays, the Senate sits as a trial body. It continues sitting until the trial is concluded—though it can take up other Senate business, under special procedures, during trial days.

The House managers, acting as prosecutors, make an opening statement, question and cross-examine witnesses, argue matters of procedure and make a closing statement. The attorneys for the President, on the other side, perform a similar function.

What happens if a President invokes executive privilege in refusing to make information available to the Senate? According to a recent Justice department statement, "a constitutional confrontation of the highest magnitude" would arise if the President refused on the grounds of national security. The Department said it was not aware of any

Federal impeachment effort where executive privilege
was invoked. There are thus virtually no precedents to serve
as a guide to Senate action, say authorities, that could possibly involve contempt citations and even arrests of witnesses in the Capitol building itself.

Do the Senators engage in debate during the trial? Not
during the taking of testimony, which is open to the public.
They may submit questions in writing, however, to the
Chief Justice, who then puts the questions to witnesses.
However, shortly before any vote on conviction is taken, a
closed session of the Senate is held, with the public barred.
At that time, Senators may debate the issue, usually under
a fifteen-minute time limit for each member. Unlimited debate—opening the possibility of a filibuster—is not allowed.

How is the deciding vote taken? At the end of the trial,
a yea and nay vote—that is, a recorded vote—is taken on
each article of impeachment when requested by the House
managers. If the President is convicted by a two-thirds vote
of those present on any one article of impeachment, he is
removed from office.

*Even if a President is found guilty of only one charge
out of five, say, he is removed from office?* That is right. A
certified copy of the judgment is deposited with the Secretary of State.

If a President Is Convicted

*In case of conviction, when does a President actually
leave office?* He is out of office immediately. The Vice President becomes President as soon as he can be sworn in.

Is there any appeal from conviction? Not according to
most authorities. Some legal experts argue that if there
were lack of due process of law during the trial itself, a
President could appeal to the Supreme Court on those
grounds. However, the weight of reasoning by legal scholars
is very heavy against this argument.

Can a President be further punished by the Senate? Yes.
Under the Constitution, the Senate may disqualify him

from holding "any office of honor, trust or profit under the United States."

Would a President who had been convicted by the Senate still be subject to trial on criminal charges in a court of law? Yes. Article I, Section 3 of the Constitution states: "The party convicted shall nevertheless be liable and subject to indictment, trial, judgment and punishment, according to law."

Does a convicted President qualify for a Government pension? Under a law passed in 1958 he could not draw a pension for his presidential service. However, a President might be entitled to a Government pension for other Federal service, such as being a member of Congress, before he became Chief Executive.

WHAT IS AN IMPEACHABLE OFFENSE? [3]

President Nixon does not have to be guilty of an indictable criminal offense to be impeached, concluded the staff of the House Judiciary committee last week. The committee's Democratic chairman, Peter Rodino of New Jersey, concurred, "This is the view I've had all along."

That is nonsense, countered Edward Hutchinson of Michigan, the senior Republican member of the committee. "There should be criminality involved [for a President to be impeached]." Hutchinson said of the staff report's conclusion, "I do not endorse it." The Rodino-Hutchinson difference is not a purely partisan disagreement, however.

Whatever the views of the Democratic majority on the committee, several of the sixteen other Republicans agree with Hutchinson, but several—in varying degrees—do not. This early split over the first major question that the committee will face—the definition of what constitutes an impeachable offense by a President—points up the problem

[3] "House Committee Debates an 'Impeachable Offense,' " by James R. Dickenson. *National Observer*. p 2. Mr. 2, '74. Reprinted with permission from *The National Observer*, copyright Dow Jones & Company, Inc. 1974.

faced by a Republican congressman investigating a Republican President. If he ultimately supports impeachment, a GOP congressman risks alienating his hard-core party support; if he votes against it, he risks offending the independent and Democratic support he may need back home.

"He Is a Principled . . . Conservative"

This dilemma confronts partisans of both sides during impeachment proceedings partly because the targets of such proceedings have always sought to limit charges as narrowly as possible to criminal offenses. That was true of Republican Andrew Johnson in 1868 and of liberal Democratic Supreme Court Justice William O. Douglas in 1970.

None of the dissident Republicans on the Judiciary committee raises any question of Hutchinson's motives and sincerity. "He is a principled and intelligent conservative," says Tom Railsback of Illinois, who holds a "broader" view of impeachable offenses than Hutchinson.

But Railsback and others believe that some Republican leaders want the GOP committee members to help protect Nixon. "There's a disagreement over our roles as well as what constitutes the 'high crimes and misdemeanors' mentioned in the Constitution as impeachable offenses," he said. "My position is that we are not to act as the President's defenders, just as the Democrats shouldn't be his prosecutors."

Some other GOP committee members, such as William Cohen of Maine, also a broad constructionist on impeachable offenses, agree with Railsback. More conservative Republicans, however, think they need to stick together for self-protection against the committee Democrats, a disproportionate number of whom are liberals and ultraliberals.

"There are more hanging Democrats on this committee than there are of us," says one such Republican. Adds another, Harold Froehlich of Wisconsin, "I'm a little disappointed that the Republicans aren't sticking together a little better." Some complain that Hutchinson doesn't exert enough leadership since he believes the impeachment decision is an individual matter. Others say Railsback tries to exert influence, but holds too broad a view on what is an impeachable offense to be a spokesman for Republicans.

The twenty-one Democrats on the committee probably do have a better consensus than the Republicans partly because their task—investigating a President of the opposing party—is a little easier. The Republicans, says one GOP committee member, can be roughly divided into three groups of varying degrees of partisanship.

The most partisan are Froehlich, David Dennis of Indiana (who is regarded by members of both parties as the best lawyer on the committee), Carlos Moorhead of California, Trent Lott of Mississippi, Lawrence Hogan of Maryland, and Delbert Latta of Ohio. Latta is a conservative who just joined the committee to replace William Keating, who resigned, and the choice of Latta by the House GOP leadership interests committee members.

"He's a strong conservative to help protect the President," says a Democratic committee member, William Hungate of Missouri. Republicans agree. "The powers that be in the party want a safe vote for the President," says one. "It's an attempt to pack the committee," says another.

There Are Shades of Difference

The next group, somewhat less partisan, includes Hutchinson, Charles Wiggins of California, Wiley Mayne of Iowa, M. Caldwell Butler of Virginia, and Charles Sandman Jr., and Joseph Maraziti of New Jersey. The third group—generally broad constructionists—includes Railsback, Cohen, Henry Smith 3d and Hamilton Fish Jr. of New York, and, to a lesser degree, Robert McClory of Illinois.

There are shades of difference, however. Dennis may be one of the most partisan Republicans, but he considers it "at least debatable that it [the requirement for impeachment] has to be an indictable offense, but it has to be a very serious offense. Most such offenses probably involve some criminality." Likewise, McClory, the second most senior Republican, would include as an impeachable offense "grossly unethical or unfaithful conduct while in office." Since the most serious charges against Nixon involve criminality [alleged bribery in the milk-fund case, obstruction of justice in the Watergate cover-up], McClory considers himself essentially in agreement with Hutchinson.

Hutchinson may not be one of the most partisan Republicans, but his adamant stand makes him a good spokesman for them. "Impeachment has to be for an indictable crime," he argues. "And we have to have evidence that will convict beyond a reasonable doubt, not probable cause that a crime was committed and that the President did it. My responsibility is not simply to pass the buck to the Senate."

The committee must apply the standards of law, "not public events because that's acting politically," Hutchinson adds. He also believes that the sentiment for impeachment is generated by a hostile press. "The press is trying to knock this President out of office. The people wish the press would get off it—impeach him or get off his back."

Hutchinson has considerable support from men such as Wiggins, Butler, and Hogan, who argue that impeachment must be based on criminal offenses to command public support. "You risk civil disorder if a majority of the people don't want the President removed," Wiggins contends.

The staff report, however, argues that: "The criminal law sets a general standard of conduct which all must follow. It does not address itself to the abuses of presidential power. In an impeachment proceeding a President is called to account for abusing powers which only a President possesses."

The report says impeachable offenses include, "conduct undermining the integrity of office, disregard of constitutional duties and oath of office, arrogation of power, abuse of the governmental process, and adverse impact on the system of government." The report implied that Nixon could be held accountable for the bombing of Cambodia, impoundment of funds, the actions of subordinates, and the firing of Archibald Cox as special Watergate prosecutor.

These charges will not get much support from any of the Republican members, however, even the broadest constructionists. They consider the most serious charges to be obstruction of justice (the Watergate cover-up and missing and damaged White House tapes), bribery (the ITT and milk-producers campaign contributions if they were made in return for governmental favors, and charges of offering the directorship of the FBI to the judge who was presiding over the trial for the burglary of the office of Daniel Ellsberg's former psychiatrist), the "plumbers'" operations that investigated news leaks, and accusations that Nixon was personally, directly involved in these matters.

The White House is preparing its own brief arguing that impeachment can only be undertaken for indictable crimes. The Justice department [February 1974] issued a report saying that the definition of an impeachable offense is unresolved. The study says the language of the Constitution supports the view that a President may be impeached only for an indictable crime. But the study says debate during the writing and ratification of the Constitution lends weight to the view that the President may be impeached for serious but noncriminal misconduct.

CHARGING THE PRESIDENT'S MEN [4]

Reprinted from *U.S. News & World Report*

A Federal grand jury reached high into the ranks of the Nixon Administration on March 1 [1974] with the criminal indictments of seven persons in the Watergate case.

The indictments, capping twenty months of intensive investigation, were the most massive charges of criminal acts by high officials in the nation's history.

Along with the indictments, a sealed "report and recom-

[4] "Charges Against White House." *U.S. News & World Report.* 76:21-4. Mr. 11, '74.

mendation" was given to United States District Court Judge John J. Sirica. The judge read it to himself, then resealed it, saying he would hold it in his custody "until further order."

There was speculation that the secret report might deal with the question of whether Mr. Nixon was personally aware of the Watergate conspiracy which the indictments alleged.

One theory: the report might eventually be sent to the House Judiciary committee for its use in deciding whether Mr. Nixon should be impeached.

Blow to President?

Almost immediately, the President's foes seized on the grand-jury action, claiming it could be a serious blow to Richard Nixon's fight to escape impeachment by the House of Representatives.

Those indicted included four former White House aides, a former Attorney General, a former Assistant Attorney General, and a lawyer for the Committee for the Re-election of the President, which ran the 1972 campaign.

All were accused of conspiracy to obstruct justice by attempts to cover up responsibility for the break-in and bugging of Democratic headquarters in Washington's Watergate complex on June 17, 1972. All but one were charged specifically with obstructing justice. And four faced additional charges of making false statements or committing perjury. Those indicted, and the charges made against them, are:

John N. Mitchell, former Attorney General and twice manager of Nixon presidential campaigns, charged with one count of conspiracy, one count of obstructing justice, two counts of making false declarations to a grand jury, one count of making a false statement to agents of the Federal Bureau of Investigation, and one count of perjury before the Senate's Watergate investigating committee

H. R. Haldeman, former chief of the Nixon White House staff, accused on one count of conspiracy, one count of obstructing justice, and three counts of perjury before the Senate committee

John D. Ehrlichman, once the President's top White House adviser on domestic affairs, indicted on one count of conspiracy, one of obstructing justice, one of making false statements to FBI agents, and two counts of making a false declaration to a grand jury

Gordon Strachan, a staff assistant to Mr. Haldeman at the White House, accused on one count of conspiracy, one of obstructing justice and one of making a false declaration to a grand jury

Charles W. Colson, who was a special counsel to the President, indicted on one count of conspiracy and one count of obstructing justice

Kenneth W. Parkinson, an attorney for the Nixon re-election committee, accused of conspiracy and of obstructing justice

Robert C. Mardian, once an assistant attorney general and later a campaign aide, accused only of conspiracy. He was the only one not charged with specific acts to obstruct justice.

All the charges listed in the indictments carry maximum sentences of five years in prison and fines ranging from $2,000 for perjury through $5,000 for conspiracy or obstructing justice, to $10,000 for making false statements.

Leon Jaworski, the special prosecutor in charge of the grand jury's investigations, told Judge Sirica that the trials will probably take three or four months. And the grand jury—which was empaneled on June 5, 1972—was told it might be asked to return to work later. The significance of that instruction was not explained, but could indicate further investigations or indictments.

The whole proceedings lasted only twelve minutes before an audience of some 60 news reporters, members of the grand jury of 14 men and 9 women, and lawyers of the special prosecutor's staff.

"The President's Hope—"

The White House issued a statement saying:

The President has always maintained that the judicial system is the proper forum for the resolution of the questions concerning Watergate.

The indictments indicate that the judicial process is finally moving toward resolution of the matter. It is the President's hope that the trials will move quickly to a just conclusion.

The President is confident that all Americans will join him in recognizing that those indicted are presumed innocent unless proof of guilt is established in the courts.

Arraignment of the seven defendants was set for March 9.

Total of Thirty-six

These latest indictments brought to thirty-six the number of people who have been accused of crimes as a result of investigations related to or growing out of the Watergate case. In the original Watergate trial of January 1973, seven men were convicted or pleaded guilty of complicity in the break-in itself.

The new indictments deal with subsequent attempts to cover up the circumstances of that break-in.

The indictments, filling fifty pages, told in detail a story of alleged lies, deceptions and repeated attempts to thwart official investigations.

All this was done, in the words of the indictment, "for the purpose of concealing and causing to be concealed the identities of the persons who were responsible for, participated in, and had knowledge of (a) the activities which were the subject of the [Watergate] investigation and trial; and (b) other illegal and improper activities."

The grand jury listed forty-five specific "overt acts," including:

Altering, destroying or concealing documents and records

Paying $557,500 in "cash funds" to the seven original defendants

Making offers of clemency to four of those defendants

Trying to obtain financial aid from the Central Intelligence Agency (CIA) for the Watergate defendants

Seeking to obstruct investigations by the Federal Bureau of Investigation and the Department of Justice

Trying to enlist the aid of the then-Attorney General, Richard Kleindienst, in obtaining the release of one or more of those arrested at the Watergate break-in in 1972

According to the indictment: John Mitchell met with Mr. Mardian in California on the day of the break-in and asked him to tell G. Gordon Liddy, a campaign aide, "to seek the assistance" of Mr. Kleindienst. Mr. Liddy was later convicted in the original Watergate trial of January 1973.

Mr. Mitchell was accused of making false statements to investigators that "he had no knowledge of the break-in . . . other than what he had read in newspaper accounts."

Another Charge

The former Attorney General also was accused of falsely telling a grand jury that he had no knowledge of clandestine activities to spy on the Democratic party or any of its candidates.

In testifying before the Senate committee, the indictment alleged, Mr. Mitchell lied in denying that he had heard of the so-called Gemstone files which, according to Senate-committee witnesses, contained the results of wiretapping the Democratic headquarters.

Mr. Haldeman was accused of lying to the Senate committee by saying that "no one, to my knowledge, was aware" that campaign-committee funds were used for purposes that "involved either blackmail or 'hush money' until the suggestion was raised in March of 1973."

It was at that time, Mr. Nixon has said, that he first became aware that he had not been getting the truth about a White House cover-up.

A charge that could prove significant in impeachment investigations of President Nixon was that Mr. Haldeman lied in his account of a conversation in the President's office on March 21, 1973.

John W. Dean 3d, former counsel to the President, told the Senate committee that in that conversation Mr. Nixon said it would be "no problem" to raise the million dollars which Mr. Dean said Watergate defendants were demanding.

"It Would Be Wrong"

Mr. Haldeman testified that what Mr. Nixon actually said was: "There is no problem in raising a million dollars, we can do that, but it would be wrong."

According to the grand jury—which had access to a tape recording of that conversation—Mr. Haldeman knew he was lying when he quoted the President as saying "but it would be wrong."

Mr. Ehrlichman's charges of making false declarations to a grand jury were based on:

Assertions that he did not know when he first learned about the involvement of Mr. Liddy in the Watergate break-in or who told him about it

Denials that he approved the purpose for which money raised by Mr. Nixon's personal attorney, Herbert W. Kalmbach, was to be used or that he told Mr. Kalmbach to keep the money-raising a secret because it would be "political dynamite" if it ever got out

The money allegedly was used for the Watergate defendants, their families and their attorneys.

Mr. Strachan was charged with making false statements that he acted on his own initiative when he took $350,000 from Mr. Haldeman's safe and gave it to a campaign official.

Mr. Parkinson's alleged role in the conspiracy was described in these words:

"In or about mid-July 1972, John N. Mitchell and Kenneth W. Parkinson met with John W. Dean . . . at which time Mitchell advised Dean to obtain FBI reports of the investigation into the Watergate break-in for Parkinson and others."

Mr. Colson was accused of participating in discussions about payments to Watergate defendants and of being advised by Mr. Dean not to send a revealing memo to investigating authorities.

The name of Mr. Dean appeared repeatedly in incidents cited in the indictments. But he was not one of the persons indicted because he has already pleaded guilty to a charge of obstructing justice and is awaiting sentence. He is expected to testify for the Government in forthcoming trials.

Mr. Dean was the only witness before the Senate investigating committee to link Mr. Nixon directly with the cover-up—telling the committee that he left Mr. Nixon's office after a conversation on September 15, 1972, convinced that the President "was well aware" of what was going on.

Besides Mr. Dean, others who have pleaded guilty to conspiracy to obstruct justice are Frederick C. LaRue and Jeb Stuart Magruder, both of whom served in the White House as well as on the Nixon campaign staff. . . . [Magruder's sentence was 10 months to 4 years; LaRue's was deferred.]

Pleas of Guilty

Herbert W. Kalmbach, Mr. Nixon's personal attorney, has pleaded guilty to campaign-fund violations, and Herbert L. Porter, a campaign aide, has pleaded guilty to a charge of making a false statement to the FBI. Dwight L. Chapin, the President's former appointments secretary, faces trial on April 1 on a charge of false testimony to a grand jury. [Mr. Chapin was convicted on April 5, 1974, and sentenced in May to six months in jail.—Ed.]

Egil Krogh, head of a group known as "the plumbers,"

assigned to investigate leaks of secret information, has pleaded guilty to directing a break-in of a psychiatrist's office in 1971 to obtain records of Daniel Ellsberg, then a defendant in the Pentagon Papers case. [Mr. Krogh was sentenced to six months in prison on January 24, 1974.—Ed.]

Mr. Ehrlichman and two others—David Young and G. Gordon Liddy—await trial for their alleged roles in that raid.

Two Nixon campaign workers—Donald H. Segretti and George A. Hearing—have pleaded guilty to so-called dirty tricks—illegally distributing false campaign literature.

Eight business executives have been charged with making illegal campaign contributions from corporate funds—seven of whom were fined, with one awaiting trial.

Rounding out this long list of Watergate casualties are the four defendants in the so-called Vesco case.

Mr. Mitchell and former Commerce Secretary Maurice Stans were put on trial in that case in New York on February 19, charged with seeking to sidetrack a Federal investigation of New Jersey financier Robert Vesco in return for a large campaign contribution. [Mr. Mitchell and Mr. Stans were acquitted of all charges by a Federal district court jury in New York City April 28.—Ed.]

Besides the grand jury which produced the March 1 indictments, two other Federal grand juries are at work investigating other allegations growing out of the 1972 campaign.

Among subjects under study by those grand juries:

The activities of the White House "plumbers" unit

The cause of an eighteen-and-one-half-minute gap in a key White House tape recording subpoenaed as grand-jury evidence

The so-called milk-fund case, in which investigators seek a possible link between campaign contributions by milk producers and an increase in milk-price supports granted by the Nixon Administration after first rejecting it

Another campaign-contribution case, which involves the International Telephone & Telegraph Company (The issue there: An antitrust suit against ITT was settled out of court after ITT pledged to contribute heavily toward cost of the 1972 Republican National Convention.)

Link Denied

Administration officials have denied any link between the campaign offers and subsequent Government actions in the milk-fund or ITT cases.

The tape-gap mystery was handed to a grand jury after a panel of technical experts told a Federal court that only repeated hand operations of a recorder could have erased the missing portion of what prosecutors believe was a key conversation about Watergate.

The White House has challenged the experts' conclusion and hired another expert to test a theory that the erasure could have been produced accidentally by a malfunctioning recorder.

No date was set for starting the trials of the seven indicted for the Watergate cover-up. But Special Prosecutor Jaworski asked that they be expedited and especially assigned to a specific judge instead of going into the normal rotation pool of several judges.

Judge Sirica, who had presided over the original Watergate trial, promptly assigned the trials to himself. Although he will soon step down—because of age—as chief judge of the United States District Court for the District of Columbia, he will remain on as a trial judge.

Assertions of Innocence

Several of those indicted were quick to assert their innocence.

Mr. Colson told a news conference: "I know that in the end my innocence will be established" and declared he was "proud to have served a man [Mr. Nixon] whom I believe history will record as one of the greatest and most courageous of our Presidents."

Mr. Parkinson issued a statement predicting that "my innocence will be clearly demonstrated."

With the long-awaited cover-up indictments out of the way—and the resulting trials not expected until spring or early summer—attention shifted back to the congressional battle over impeachment of the President.

Now, the sealed report given Judge Sirica by the grand jury has added a new element of mystery to that conflict.

Mr. Jaworski, according to informed sources, had decided not to seek Mr. Nixon's indictment—or even his personal testimony—but to leave his case to Congress, which he considered the proper forum for proceedings against a President. He had also expressed the belief that he could not turn over grand-jury evidence to congressional investigators without authorization from a court.

THE POWER TO SUBPOENA [5]

The House of Representatives voted 410 to 4 today to grant the Judiciary committee broad constitutional power to investigate President Nixon's conduct. The House thus formally ratified the impeachment inquiry begun by the committee last October [1973] and empowered the panel to subpoena anyone, including the President, with evidence pertinent to the investigation.

It was only the second time in the nation's history that such a step, directed at a President, had been taken in the House. But the roll-call vote was not a test of impeachment sentiment.

The vote followed an hour of debate in which no one rose to defend Mr. Nixon, but Democrats and Republicans quarreled over the best method to guarantee that the inquiry would not become partisan.

[5] "House, 410-4, Gives Subpoena Power in Nixon Inquiry," article by James M. Naughton, of the New York *Times* Washington Bureau. New York *Times*. p 1+. F. 7, '74. © 1974 by The New York Times Company. Reprinted by permission.

"No Other Way"

The tone was struck by the Judiciary committee chairman, Representative Peter W. Rodino Jr., Democrat of New Jersey, when he told an unusually attentive House:

Whatever the result, whatever we learn or conclude, let us now proceed with such care and decency and thoroughness and honor that the vast majority of the American people, and their children after them, will say: This was the right course. There was no other way.

The four members who opposed the resolution, all Republicans, were Ben B. Blackburn of Georgia, Earl F. Landgrebe of Indiana, Carlos J. Moorhead of California and David C. Treen of Louisiana.

Mr. Moorhead, a member of the Judiciary committee, objected that the resolution gave the panel such unrestricted subpoena power that it "can only precipitate a constitutional confrontation and further divide the people of our country."

The significance of the House action was illustrated by Mr. Rodino's statement that the power to issue and enforce a subpoena would be drawn directly from the Constitution, and would "not depend upon any statutory provisions or require judicial enforcement."

He said that a subpoena would be issued to Mr. Nixon only if the committee thought it necessary to reach a "fair" judgment whether there were grounds for impeachment.

"The gentleman from New Hampshire hopes that will not be necessary," Representative Louis C. Wyman, Republican of New Hampshire, said as he stared across the quiet chamber at Mr. Rodino.

"The gentleman from New Jersey does also," Mr. Rodino replied.

He told newsmen later that no decisions would be made within the next few days on requests for evidence to either the White House or to the Watergate special prosecutor, Leon Jaworski.

The resolution was adopted after the House rejected, 342 to 70, a parliamentary effort to open the measure to amendments that would have set an April 30 deadline for completion of the inquiry and allowed the committee's senior Republican to issue subpoenas independently.

"Good With Me"

Representative John J. Rhodes of Arizona, the House Republican leader, signaled the fate of the parliamentary maneuver when he declared that Mr. Rodino's pledge to conduct the inquiry fairly and expeditiously was "good with me."

Only 67 of 178 Republicans voting on the issue and 3 of 234 Democrats disagreed and sought unsuccessfully adoption of the restrictions.

As approved, the measure . . . [provides] no termination date for the investigation. It authorized Mr. Rodino and the ranking Republican, Representative Edward Hutchinson of Michigan, to issue subpoenas jointly. If either declines, the full committee, composed of 21 Democrats and 17 Republicans, must decide whether to issue a subpoena.

Representative Robert McClory, Republican of Illinois, asserted that a fixed deadline would assure a troubled nation that the Watergate turmoil would soon end.

"Imagine!" he protested, his voice and arms rising and falling together. "Imagine this important resolution, historic in its impact, being presented here without an opportunity for amendment."

Representative William L. Hungate, Democrat of Missouri, retorted dryly that it would be irresponsible to set an "arbitrary" deadline that might put the committee in "the position of the skydiver whose chute failed to open and found he had jumped to a conclusion."

Several Republicans warned that the inquiry could degenerate into partisanship without a guarantee that the Democratic majority would not suppress a subpoena written by the senior Republican.

"Suppose we wanted to call [Senator] Hubert Humphrey or Bobby Baker?" asked Representative David W. Dennis, Republican of Indiana. Mr. Baker was convicted in 1967 of larceny, fraud and income tax evasion after an inquiry into his activities as the secretary to Senate Democrats.

Republicans apparently took their cue, however, from Mr. Rhodes, who said that the minority would be able to "look at its options" later if the inquiry became partisan.

Despite the seriousness of the House action, there was no indication of influence having been exerted either by the White House or by groups lobbying on behalf of the impeachment of Mr. Nixon.

The President had breakfast at the White House this morning with thirty-seven Republican senators and representatives who are members of two informal Capitol Hill groups, the Chowder and Marching Society and the S.O.S Club. Only four of Mr. Nixon's House guests supported the effort to amend the resolution, and none of them opposed its final approval.

The House has taken formal impeachment action only a dozen times before. The only instance in which a President's conduct was investigated was in 1867, when the House adopted a similar resolution directing the Judiciary committee to inquire into the possible impeachment of Andrew Johnson.

Equally "Solemn"

The House rejected the committee's articles of impeachment in December 1867, but voted two months later to impeach President Johnson after he dismissed Secretary of War Edward M. Stanton. The Senate subsequently acquitted Johnson.

Referring to the Johnson impeachment, Mr. Rhodes described the House proceeding today as an equally "solemn occasion."

What the House concludes in Mr. Nixon's case, said

Representative Elizabeth Holtzman, Democrat of Brooklyn, "will stand for all time. We will act expeditiously, but we will act soundly."

Mr. Rodino also referred to the need for sensitivity and caution.

"For almost two hundred years," he said, "Americans have undergone the stress of preserving their freedom and the Constitution that protects it. It is our turn now."

GOING TO THE PEOPLE [6]

It was the biggest gamble of Richard Nixon's quarter century in American politics—a desperate and perhaps doomed attempt to buy his survival as President at the forfeit of his public and personal reputation. His play was the public surrender of 1,254 pages and 200,000 words of transcripts of his secret Watergate tapes; he hoped, improbably, that they would clear him. But what Mr. Nixon demonstrated instead was why he had fought so long to suppress them.

Even as edited by the White House, the transcripts portrayed Mr. Nixon himself as a weak, profane, cynical, isolated, inept and finally amoral leader of men. They shredded decades of public protestations of probity; they made a mockery of claims to "law and order." At their very worst they painted the President of the United States as a party to a criminal conspiracy—a $75,000 hush-money payment designed, in his own words, to "keep the cap on" the scandals threatening to bring down his presidency.

The Nixon Papers thus stood as the most extraordinary in the history of the American presidency—a bowdlerized but still brutally revealing glimpse into the sort of *realpolitik* practiced by Mr. Nixon to cling to power and keep his people out of prison. His plain intent in publishing them was to blunt the accelerating House impeachment inquiry and to bury Watergate in a blizzard of paper, enough

[6] From "A Desperate Gamble for Survival." *Newsweek.* 83:17+. My. 13, '74. Copyright Newsweek, Inc. 1974, reprinted by permission.

at least to raise reasonable doubts as to his own technical liability to a felony charge. If the cost was his final humiliation before the governed, so be it. "You can't impeach him," said one staffer hopefully, "for thinking bad thoughts."

The first public and political reaction to the acres of newsprint was indeed numb and muted. But even before the full impact was felt, a Gallup telephone poll of 694 households returned a heavy 62-24 majority against accepting the President's offer of edited tapes instead of transcripts. And the first fragmentary revelations wounded him badly: 42 percent of the sampling thought less of Mr. Nixon as a result, to 35 who felt no differently—and 17 who contrived to like him better than ever.

And as the week wore on, the cumulative effect was devastating. House Majority Leader Thomas P. (Tip) O'Neill told a Republican colleague privately that a bill of impeachment, far from suffocating under the mass of transcripts, would carry by one hundred votes. Even some of Mr. Nixon's own employees were appalled by what the record told about the boss; reading parts of it, said one, was "like being electrocuted in the bathtub." Another senior hand conceded bleakly: "We have a . . . disaster on our hands."

The potential danger was redoubled by Mr. Nixon's signaled determination to stand on the transcripts and stonewall any further demands for evidence. His expurgated evidence placed him in defiance of a House Judiciary committee subpoena for tapes or other first-hand records of forty-two White House conversations. The committee so notified him, but decided not to wait for an answer; it will at last begin its hearings on the impeachment case against Richard Nixon—a case that can only be strengthened if the White House defies lawful requests for evidence. The President at the same time moved to quash an overlapping subpoena by Special Prosecutor Leon Jaworski for 64 conversations—20 of them included among the transcripts, 44 left out. The struggle could lead to a full-blown constitutional collision in the Supreme Court, and perhaps worse. "We haven't," one Jaworski aide said wanly, "ruled out the possibility of another Saturday Night Massacre."

The Nixon Papers fell short of the minimal demands for evidence. They were, for one thing, a patchy job of work: 11 of the 42 conversations under House subpoena were reported nonexistent or missing, and the typescript record that survived was shot through with nearly two thousand omissions marked "inaudible," "unintelligible," "expletive deleted," or "material unrelated to presidential action." And, damning as they seemed, they covered only a fraction of the metastatic spread of scandals around the Nixon presidency. Mr. Nixon, in his selection of tapes and in his presentation speech, unilaterally narrowed the scope of the impeachment case to the Watergate break-in and cover-up; his people said they would resist a Judiciary request for 142 more conversations covering the ITT and milk-fund cases as well. In his reduced state, his recalcitrance was widely taken to mean that the worst was yet to come. If material like this was released, "Can you imagine what's in the stuff he's holding back?" said a Justice department official. "It must be dynamite."

What he yielded up was dynamite enough. Mr. Nixon tried to tamp down its explosive potential, first in his prime-time television speech, next morning in a best-case legal brief crafted by his lawyers. He conceded in advance that the papers would subject him to suspicion, embarrassment, "even ridicule"; he acknowledged having tried to do not only what was moral but what was politic; he agreed that the transcripts were open to interpretations that might be "drastically different" from his own. But, he went on, he was publishing them anyway, "blemishes and all," because he had confidence that the record as a whole would prove his innocence. They would show, he said, that he was ignorant of the Watergate cover-up till John Dean told him about it on March 21, 1973, and that he had tried diligently thereafter to uncover it. The case, in his telling, came down to his word against Dean's; the record would show Dean a liar—and Mr. Nixon a man "trying . . . to discover what was right and to do what was right."

Precious little in the released papers bore him out. They faulted Dean's morals, but not his memory for essential detail—and not his basic accusations as to the practice of law and order in the Oval Office. What emerged instead was a savagely unflattering portrait of Mr. Nixon decreeing the use of the FBI to hound his political enemies; advising his senior staffers that "perjury is a hard rap to prove" and that one can safely forget facts before a grand jury; listening with evident equanimity to reports that various of his people had in fact lied to protect him; agreeing with Dean's wry wish that the White House had the Mafia's skill at laundering silence money; scheming to set up his friend and first-term Attorney General John Mitchell to take the fall for everybody; and trying to pressure Dean into silence by denying him immunity from prosecution—or to tempt him into it with an oblique promise of a pardon if he got in trouble.

Most of all, the Nixon Papers gave the lie to one presidential statement after another that his single concern was to get out the truth. Publication day fell fortuitously a year to the day after the scandal cracked wide open and Mr. Nixon declared himself "determined that we should get to the bottom of the matter . . . no matter who was involved." But as the transcripts richly reveal, the pervasive concern instead was to contain the damage and shelter the President; telling the whole truth was only intermittently and fleetingly considered among the options toward that end. Early on, when Dean tentatively suggested it, Mr. Nixon answered flatly: "We have passed that point." . . .

"Out Front" of the Scandal

Laying so destructive a self-portrait out on public view had the look, in hindsight, of a badly miscalculated risk.

The transcripts themselves reveal a strain of wistful thinking among Mr. Nixon and his inner council, a kind of
constant groping for that one PR coup that would get them
"out front" or "on top" or "ahead of the curve"; even as
the scandal was engulfing him, the President himself once
mused aloud that it would all be over after "a horrible two
weeks" if they could make a sacrifice of Mitchell. That
train of thought persists around the Nixon White House,
and in fact helped tip the balance toward public disclosure,
as against, say, a discreet private delivery to the committee
and the attendant risk that the worst of it would leak out
piecemeal. "We didn't think it was going to get the reception of 'Gone With the Wind,' " said White House staffer
Patrick Buchanan; still, the bet was that the Nixon Papers
would last three or four days on page one and then die.

The larger miscalculation still was that the transcripts
would, for all their ambiguities, clear the President. The
problem was that he and his tiny circle of advisers had focused on the wrong charges against him—that he had fore-
knowledge of the Watergate break-in and that he was thoroughly wired into the cover-up long before March 21. The
transcripts were helpful, though hardly conclusive, on both
counts. But the decisive question in the impeachment inquiry now is what he knew and what he did on and after
the 21st, not before; it is precisely in that period that the
papers were most devastating, both to his image and to his
legal defense.

The decision was in the end the President's own—one
he reached after a long passage of what one aide called
"near agony" suffered in that solitude he has always sought
out in his crises. His options, with the House and Jaworski
subpoenas upon him, were narrow. Total capitulation once
again was not seriously among them, and straight-out defiance was no longer viable. But reducing the tapes to tran-
script form gave him some control over their presentation,
and making them public did have a certain short-term PR
genius—a grand-scale coming-clean that would at least brace

up his faltering GOP support and slow the pell-mell plunge toward impeachment.

As early as mid-April, he tried out the idea on Nelson Rockefeller in a private audience, confiding that he planned to "shoot the works, get the story out. . . . By the time I finish, I'll have them." With the subpoena coming due, he retired to Camp David with his yellow pads, a relay of secretaries and finally staffer Ray Price, who writes his soft-line speeches—and . . . he came home with his decision.

Hours before telecast time, his people previewed his plan to some presumptively friendly audiences, to decidely mixed notices. White House chief of staff Alexander Haig ran a draft of the speech past the Republican leadership; they were greatly pleased at the bottom line but appalled at the three pages flailing out at the media, the Judiciary committee and its staff lawyers for being out to "get" the President. "This is the *old* Nixon—defiant, combative, challenging," protested House GOP leader John Rhodes. "We can't support this speech." Haig, taken aback, went to see the President alone and reappeared fifteen minutes later with his assent to drop the offending language.

Next Haig and defense lawyer James St. Clair outlined the proposition to the Cabinet, even playing a two- or three-minute snippet of particularly staticky tape to demonstrate how inaudible the "inaudibles" really can be. Once again, the response was general relief at the President's decision— but the first and most frequent query at question time was why it had taken him so long.

"The Rough and the Smooth"

The speech as performance was masterfully done—perhaps the best in a year's presidential utterances on the scandals. Mr. Nixon's hair was freshly trimmed for the occasion, and the Oval Office thermostat was turned low to keep him from sweating; the transcripts were stacked up theatrically on a table beside him, bound in green plastic loose-leaf covers to heighten the appearance of sheer bulk.

They contained, he said early on, "everything that is relevant" to the Watergate case—"the rough as well as the smooth." If Judiciary had any doubts as to their authenticity, chairman Peter W. Rodino and ranking Republican Edward Hutchinson (though not their staff lawyers) could come around, listen to the tapes and discuss any complaints about deletions with Mr. Nixon himself. But the only fair judgment as to their content, in Mr. Nixon's telling, was "that the President has nothing to hide."

Much of the talk was an apologia in advance for what the transcripts would show—the "uninhibited discussion" and "brutal candor"; the "ambiguities" that would surely be held against him by his "political and journalistic opponents"; his own manifest concern for handling the Watergate mess "in a way that would cause the least unnecessary [political] damage." Against that vast bulk, he cobbled up his own highly selective sampler of quotations that, wrenched from context, flattered his cause: "We all have to do the right thing, we just cannot have this kind of business. . . . Tell the truth, that is the thing I have told everybody around here." At the close, he begged the merciful judgment of the nation. "The entire story is there," he said. ". . . [For] those who are willing to look at it fully, fairly and objectively, the evidence will be persuasive and, I hope, conclusive."

The speech began a major media blitz—an overnight effort to promote Mr. Nixon's gesture as a massive generosity and to frame the evidence in advance in the best possible light for him. By cautious design, the fifty-page White House brief of the evidence was delivered to the press five hours before the transcripts themselves. It portrayed Dean, without quite saying so, as a persistent perjurer and Mr. Nixon as an innocent man who may have intermittently sounded guilty simply because he was "taking the role of devil's advocate . . . [or] merely thinking out loud." The bottom line, in this benign reading, was that the President had only the most fragmentary knowledge of the cover-up before March 21 and that he "co-operated fully" in getting it before a grand jury thereafter. "In all the thousands of words spoken," said the brief, ". . . not once does it appear that the President . . . was engaged in a criminal plot to obstruct justice."

The gesture went over relatively well on the Hill, and the White House at first was euphoric—inexplicably so, given its awareness of what the papers actually contained. But as the transcripts circulated through Washington and spilled into the newspapers, the dimensions of the disaster began coming clear. Not a single ranking Republican leader except Gerald Ford could be found to advocate Mr. Nixon's innocence, despite considerable wooing by the White House, and even the Veep began backpedaling by the weekend; he conceded after a quick reading that the papers were a "disappointment" to him—a collective record that qualified no one, the President included, for sainthood.

That, as it developed, was a comparatively charitable reading; the more common reactions in political Washington were mixed depression and anger, not merely at the evidence suggesting Mr. Nixon's culpability in a crime but at the smaller-than-life portrait the papers drew of the men who ran America. The New York *Times*'s William Safire, once a Nixon speechwriter, judged him "guilty of conduct unbecoming a President." William Randolph Hearst Jr., till now an indefatigable Nixon supporter, found him "a man totally absorbed in the cheapest and sleaziest kind of conniving."

"Let Him Fly Over"

The more critical danger was the melancholic reaction among Republicans on the Hill—the party loyalists who are Mr. Nixon's last hedge against impeachment in the House and conviction by the Senate. The shadow of criminality over the White House was stunning enough; one House Republican hierarch felt sickened at the picture of a President even entertaining the notion of paying off a convicted burglar—and at having to "live with the fact that such a man is still in the White House." But the full-length portrait of the mind and morals of Richard Nixon was at least equally poisonous to his standing. Somebody asked Kansas's Senator Robert Dole if he would want *that* Richard Nixon to come out and campaign for him. "Sure," Dole shot back, "let him fly over anytime." And the corrosion spread and deepened as the full impact of the transcripts gradually hit home. "He comes through," said a Midwestern GOP leader who worked for Mr. Nixon's reelection, "as a vicious s.o.b. who shouldn't be President."

The almost certain first consequence was to speed the processes of impeachment—and quite possibly to guarantee the outcome as well. The President's offer displeased the Judiciary committee on a wide range of grounds—the missing tapes, the patchy and in some cases suspect editing, the refusal to let staff lawyers sit in on verifying the transcripts, the manifest attempt by Mr. Nixon to dictate what was or wasn't relevant to the inquiry. Still, the committee Republicans hung together in a near party-line vote of 20 to 18 to advise Mr. Nixon that he had not complied with the subpoena.

That news brought some fleeting cheer to the White House, which has been trying to show up the inquiry as a partisan Democratic vendetta. But its pleasure was likely to be short-lived. Judiciary's telegram count was running heavily against the President. "Impeach the [expletive deleted]," wired one Georgian and even loyalist Republicans on the committee were infected with gloom. The hearings on the evidence will begin roughly on schedule . . . [in May 1974], first in closed session, later on live TV. The committee agreed to let St. Clair sit in for the President, but not even his presence or his skill seemed likely to alter the outcome —a recommendation that the President be impeached.

The second-front struggle over Jaworski's subpoena will be joined in Judge John J. Sirica's courtroom . . . , with similarly dangerous potential; one Justice department official called it "a contest between a cobra and a mongoose" with the President's survival at stake. Mr. Nixon's constitutional-law consultant, Charles Alan Wright, composed another of his elegant briefs arguing for confidentiality in the presidency. But the claim sounded more threadbare than ever, given that Mr. Nixon himself had just breached it to the tune of a quarter million words, and it only quickened the prosecution's appetite to see what manner of secrets Mr. Nixon chose *not* to publish. The presumption on both sides is that Jaworski will have to fight to the Supreme Court to find out.

"The Finest President"

Mr. Nixon tried for the most part to behave as though in surrendering the transcripts he had in fact put an end to Watergate. He booked himself into a heavy campaign-style speaking tour—a cheer-up talk to the US Chamber of Commerce in Washington, a ribbon-cutting at Spokane's Expo 74 (where he greeted Governor Dan Evans as Governor Evidence) and a straight-out party pep rally in Phoenix, Arizona, in the heart of Barry Goldwater country. Phoenix was his first outing under the shadow of the transcripts, and his reception was reassuring. Goldwater welcomed him, cordially if not effusively, and Senator Paul Fannin introduced him to a cheering crowd of sixteen thousand as "the finest President in our history." "The time has now come," said Mr. Nixon, "to get Watergate behind us and get on with the business of America."

The time was not yet; the tragic fact, confirmed again by what Mr. Nixon revealed of himself . . . , was that Watergate has become America's business. The President has survived a year of scandal on the presumption of innocence, and even the transcripts left room for a skilled defense to raise reasonable doubts as to his technical guilt of a crime. But his survival on those terms will be purchased at great cost to the nation, and to himself. With the publication of the Nixon Papers his claim to power was no longer the stunning electoral mandate of 1972 but the plea for mercy of a man divested by his own words of the moral authority to govern.

VII. A PRESIDENT RESIGNS

EDITOR'S INTRODUCTION

The ending proved as momentous as the battle between the three branches of Government. Richard Nixon resigned. He is the first American President to have ever done so.

And so, the casual observer might think that the entire congressional investigation, the continual testing of constitutional provisions for checks and balances was nothing more than an exercise in futility. Not so. It is precisely because of the proceeding that Mr. Nixon had no choice but to resign. The ongoing impeachment proceedings had built an ironclad case for a Senate trial. When the Supreme Court ruled that Mr. Nixon had to give up more evidence, the ending seemed fated. Conviction in the Senate seemed inevitable. And so Mr. Nixon took the only other option left to him. He resigned.

Articles in this section deal with that swift ending. The first article is a *Newsweek* story on the Supreme Court ruling. It details how the high court ruled on Mr. Nixon's claims for executive privilege. Specifically, the Court said that while all three branches of Government are coequal, the Supreme Court has the final word on matters of law. One of Mr. Nixon's arguments had been that, since the three branches are equal, the Supreme Court does not have the right to tell the executive branch what it can or cannot do. The second point the Court made is that even a President has no right to withhold evidence needed in a criminal trial. The evidence was contained in the conversations taped in the President's office.

Separately, but not quite entirely apart from the Supreme Court's activities, the House Judiciary committee was deciding on whether or not to bring Mr. Nixon to trial. Its decision was, yes, he should be impeached. The second article in this section details how the committee voted to impeach Mr. Nixon.

What happened next has already been burned into the annals of history. In accordance with the Supreme Court decision, Mr. Nixon was now duty bound to release the subpoenaed tapes. But for some reason no one is able to explain, Mr. Nixon chose to make public three of those tapes.

The evidence on those tapes was damning. It outraged the public. It outraged Congress. It made patently clear that if Mr. Nixon stood trial before the Senate, he would be convicted by a large margin. Instead, Mr. Nixon resigned and Gerald Ford became President. All of this is described in the third article of the section.

The concluding article is an assessment. Historian Henry Steele Commager looks at the pell-mell rush of events and reaches a conclusion: the United States Constitution is alive and well. It has effectively dealt with the most serious Government crisis in the nation's history. And it has performed precisely the way the Founding Fathers intended that it should.

THE SUPREME COURT RULES [1]

It's an old adage around the Supreme Court that hard cases make bad law, and the case of the subpoenaed White House tapes seemed to be the hardest in memory. Not only were the Justices asked to explore the uncharted doctrine of executive privilege, but the tapes themselves were inextricably entwined with the impeachment of Richard Nixon —and the Court was deliberating under the repeatedly implied threat that Mr. Nixon might choose to ignore its order, thus touching off a shattering constitutional crisis.

[1] Reprint of article entitled "A Very Definitive Decision." *Newsweek*. 84:23-6. Ag. 5, '74. Copyright Newsweek, Inc. 1974, reprinted by permission.

So when the ruling was finally handed down . . . , it was designed to make as little law as possible: to be prudently narrow, solidly unanimous and as definitive as any President could ask.

Chief Justice Warren Burger himself wrote the opinion, joined by two more Nixon appointees and the five holdovers from the Warren Court. (Justice William H. Rehnquist, the fourth Nixon appointee, withdrew from the case, because of his previous service at [the Department of] Justice under John Mitchell.) In effect, Burger read the President a lesson in elementary civics, fetching back to the landmark *Marbury v. Madison* to reassert the High Court's right to define the law. Then Burger proceeded to define it, declaring that neither the doctrine of separation of powers nor the President's need for confidentiality in his office was reason enough to withhold evidence from a criminal trial. The conclusion: Mr. Nixon must "forthwith" turn over the tapes of sixty-four subpoenaed White House conversations to United States District Judge John J. Sirica so that he could determine whether they were relevant to the forthcoming Watergate cover-up trials.

The ruling did establish one modest benchmark: for the first time, the Court acknowledged that there were "constitutional underpinnings" for the presidential claim to executive privilege. Even this concession was kept as narrow as possible, avoiding any sweeping conclusions and explicitly refusing to discuss the limits of White House protection in the face of civil litigation or congressional demands for information. But whatever else it meant, Burger declared, executive privilege "cannot prevail over the fundamental demands of due process of law in the fair administration of criminal justice."

In its other conclusions, the ruling was clearly tailored to bridge the Court's widening opinion gaps and achieve unanimity. Burger did raise the startling possibility that a President might be cited for contempt of court, but promptly ducked it with the mild observation that such a

"peculiarly inappropriate" action would "engender protracted litigation." And despite having agreed to rule on
presidential counsel James St. Clair's protest that the Watergate grand jury had no right to name Mr. Nixon an unindicted coconspirator, the Justices simply reneged: they
had, they explained, "improvidently granted" their consent
in the first place. The effect of that maneuver was to leave
the President's standing in the case unchanged.

If the Justices had meant their 8-0 solidity to head off
a confrontation, it worked. After eight hours of public silence and internal seething, the White House announced
that Mr. Nixon would comply with the ruling—and two
days later St. Clair, Sirica and Special Prosecutor Leon
Jaworski had agreed on the schedule for turning over
the tapes; the question now became what was on them—
or wasn't.

It was a case that the Justices had been dreading for
a year—ever since Jaworski's predecessor, Archibald Cox,
subpoenaed for the first nine of the White House tapes disclosed in the Senate Watergate hearings. The White House
refusal of that legal demand had been overruled by the
United States Court of Appeals and seemed headed for the
High Court last October [1973] when a public convulsion
intervened: the President fired Cox and forced the resignations of Attorney General Elliot Richardson and his deputy,
William Ruckelshaus, touching off a firestorm of indigna-
tion. In the aftermath, Mr. Nixon agreed to Jaworski's appointment, gave him extraordinary autonomy and turned
over seven of the disputed tapes—disclosing, belatedly, that
two of them had never existed.

After Jaworski got indictments in the Watergate
cover-up, he issued a subpoena for sixty-four more tapes
of conversations that took place between June 20, 1972,
and June 4, 1973, all but one including the President—and
the battle was joined again. The case was headed back to
the appellate court last May [1974] when Jaworski, citing
the urgent need for a final ruling before the September 9

trial began, asked the Supreme Court to take up the controversy before it recessed for the summer. To the surprise of many, the Court agreed—reluctantly. After questioning Jaworski and St. Clair in oral arguments . . . [in July 1974], one Justice confided to a friend: "If we had our druthers, the case wouldn't be here. But here it is—and we've got to deal with it."

The following morning, the eight Justices met in the large conference room outside Burger's chambers and, for the next six hours, argued the case. The Justices, according to *Newsweek*'s sources, tilted heavily against the President from the first, but differed by degrees. William O. Douglas, William J. Brennan, Thurgood Marshall and Potter Stewart reportedly wanted a broad ruling on the entire issue of executive privilege, while Byron R. White and Lewis F. Powell wanted the opinion written on the narrowest possible legal grounds. The most troublesome area, however, was jurisdictional; while Burger and Harry A. Blackmun agreed with the majority on limiting privilege, they worried that Jaworski lacked the legal "standing" to sue his nominal boss, Mr. Nixon. But Stewart, the sources say, pointed to the liberal regulations establishing the autonomy of the prosecutor's office, and—under the President's implicit threat to defy an adverse ruling—the two Justices known in the Court as the Minnesota Twins made it unanimous.

Although Stewart apparently wrote the section of the opinion about the case's "justiciability," Burger assigned himself the rest of the task. "There is a tradition of assigning opinions to the least persuaded member of the Court on a particular issue," one Court source explained; that way, the reasoning goes, the opinion will reflect the consensus of the Court and avoid extreme views. The Justices were also aware, however, that an opinion written by Burger—Mr. Nixon's own appointee and a steady proponent of the President's views—would weigh heavily in Congress and the White House.

In the next two weeks Burger circulated his draft among the other Justices, each of them making additions, deletions and objections to the document. Douglas, who went home to Goose Prairie, Washington, a few days after the judges came to basic agreement, communicated his criticism by mail and telephone to his law clerks in the Capital. For a proceeding that involved eight individual and frequently argumentative lawyers, the negotiations progressed rapidly. "The public concern over delay is understandable," a source close to the Court . . . [said], "but it would be extraordinary and unique if the Court had written an opinion of this importance in a shorter time."

Neutral Tone Carefully Maintained

The thirty-one-page opinion was thus a committee project with a suitably neutral tone. The Court tidily retraced the subpoena's course, established St. Clair's right to appeal and affirmed that Jaworski had proved that the sixty-four tapes were relevant and that his subpoena was not "a fishing expedition." The Justices were impressed by St. Clair's argument that the tapes were inadmissible hearsay, but they noted that the liberal evidence rules governing conspiracy trials allowed the introduction of remarks not only by one defendant against another but also by an alleged coconspirator who was not himself a defendant—a pointed reference to Mr. Nixon's standing. The Justices then considered three major questions:

Can the special prosecutor sue the President? St. Clair had argued that the matter was an intramural quarrel between two officials in the executive branch and therefore not a case for the courts. But the Justices ruled that the Attorney General, with the President's permission, had issued a regulation investing the special prosecutor with "unique authority and tenure," including the "explicit power" to contest in court presidential claims of executive privilege. The Attorney General could also have amended or revoked that regulation, the Court said, "but he has not done so. . . . So long as this regulation is extant it has the force of law."

Is the President subject to the Court? Under the separation of powers doctrine, St. Clair had argued, the President's confidentiality is absolute and not subject to judicial review. But Jaworski had answered that the nation's constitutional form of government would be jeopardized "if the President, any President, is to say that the Constitution means what he says it does, and that there is no one, not even the Supreme Court, to tell him otherwise." The Justices easily agreed with Jaworski, reaching back to the *Marbury v. Madison* ruling in 1803 that "it is emphatically the province and duty of the judicial department to say what the law is." The Court added: "The 'judicial power of the United States' vested in the Federal courts . . . can no more be shared with the executive branch than the Chief Executive, for example, can share with the Judiciary the veto power, or the Congress share with the Judiciary the power to override a presidential veto."

Can presidential records be subpoenaed? To protect the public interest by preserving candor in discussions between the President and his closest aides, St. Clair had contended, all of the President's confidential communications must be held privileged. Jaworski had countered that the need for evidence in a criminal proceeding took precedence over the need for confidentiality.

Although the first President to claim that his records were privileged was Thomas Jefferson in 1807, the Supreme Court had never before formally recognized the doctrine. Now the Court declared flatly that "privilege is fundamental to the operation of Government and inextricably rooted in the separation of powers under the Constitution." But if there is no claim of a need to protect military, diplomatic or sensitive national security secrets, the Court added, the President's privilege of confidentiality must be weighed against the needs of criminal justice. "Without access to specific facts, a criminal prosecution may be totally frustrated," Burger wrote. "The President's broad interest in confidentiality of communications will not be vitiated by disclosure of a limited number of conversations preliminarily shown to have some bearing on the pending criminal cases."

The Justices concluded by admonishing Sirica to treat the subpoenaed tapes with the "high degree of respect due the President of the United States"—although they added in the next breath that in no sense was the President above the law. "Statements that meet the test of admissibility and relevance must be isolated," the Court said; "all other material must be excised" and protected from release or publication until it can be returned to the President. In selecting the relevant sections Sirica may consult with both Jaworski and St. Clair, but the final decision is his alone. The Court did, however, leave open the possibility that the White House may appeal Sirica's decisions, raising a glimmer of a chance of protracted bickering over the tapes.

"A Negotiated Document"

Constitutional-law experts agreed that the Court's opinion was cautious—"obviously a negotiated document," said Yale's Alexander Bickel—and that it was more a reaffirmation of the Court's historic role than a trail blazer. But that may have been just what the Justices had in mind. "I've said all along that the principal task of the Court in this historic case was to reduce the historic consequences of its decision," Bickel said. "And I think they succeeded."

In recognizing the constitutional basis for privilege, said Norman Dorsen of New York University, the Court "planted the seeds for future controversy." Bickel worried that the Court's recognition of Jaworski's right to sue Mr. Nixon could also prove troublesome. "If the principle goes one millimeter farther," Bickel said, "it could create new areas for judicial action. . . . Could [former Interior Secretary] Wally Hickel appealed to the Court when he was fired? The courts, not the President, could control the executive branch." But on both issues, he conceded, the opinion was properly vague.

In its principal thrust, however, the ruling won widespread legal applause. Cox, now a Harvard professor, declared that it "gives the country assurance that no President can block an independent and thoroughgoing investigation of wrongdoing high in the White House offices by claiming the right to withhold evidence merely upon his own say-so." And while the Justices steered wide of the impeachment inquiry, many authorities felt that the decision tended to bolster the House Judiciary committee's own subpoenas for presidential tapes.

The ruling was rapidly translated into practice; under the agreement reached . . . , the first twenty conversations were to be turned over to Judge Sirica . . . [within a week], with a "target date" of August 2 for yielding as many of the remaining forty-four conversations as possible. The President himself, St. Clair said, wanted to have listened to all of the tapes before turning them over, and all the tapes still had to be indexed, analyzed and duplicated so that the White House could retain copies. There were still possibilities for legal collisions. But the Supreme Court's action, by wide consensus, represented the best solution to a thorny problem. As NYU's Dorsen concluded, "In terms of history, precedent and pragmatism, the decision is right."

THE HISTORIC VOTE [2]

Wherefore Richard M. Nixon, by such conduct, warrants impeachment and trial, and removal from office.

After four garrulous days, the talking stopped. The room was silent, and so, in a sense, was a watching nation. One by one, the strained and solemn faces of the thirty-eight members of the House Judiciary committee were focused

[2] From "The Fateful Vote to Impeach." *Time.* 104:10-18. Ag. 5, '74. Reprinted by permission from *Time*, the weekly newsmagazine; copyright Time Inc.

on by the television cameras. One by one, their names were called. One by one, they cast the most momentous vote of their political lives, or of any representative of the American people in a century.

Mr. Railsback. Aye. Mr. Fish. Aye. Mr. Hogan. Aye. Mr. Butler. Aye. Mr. Cohen. Aye. Mr. Froehlich. Aye.

Thus six Republican congressmen joined all twenty-one Democrats to recommend that the House of Representatives impeach Richard M. Nixon and seek his removal from the presidency through a Senate trial. And thus the Judiciary committee climaxed seven months of agonizing inquiry into the conduct of Richard Nixon as President by approving an article of impeachment that charges he violated both his oath to protect the Constitution and his duty to take care that the laws be faithfully executed. The first of at least two articles to be considered, the article alleges that he committed multiple acts designed to obstruct justice in his attempt to conceal the origins of the June 1972 wiretap-burglary of Democratic National [Committee] headquarters and "other unlawful covert activities" carried out by those responsible for that crime.

By that historic roll-call vote, the article of impeachment was adopted, 27 to 11, by the committee at 7:07 P.M. on a warm Saturday night in Room 2141 of Washington's Rayburn Office Building. Richard Nixon became only the second President to stand so accused by a committee of Congress. The impressive bipartisan nature of the vote increased the probability that the full House of Representatives will also vote to impeach.

The impeachment action came at the end of a week in which the President's chances of completing his second term in office fell to their lowest point since the Watergate scandal first threatened his political survival. Earlier in the week, the Supreme Court ruled unanimously that Nixon had no authority to withhold tape recordings of his White House conversations from Special Prosecutor Leon Jaworski. The ruling raised the possibility that more evidence damaging to the President may become available.

The degree of bipartisanship in the Judiciary committee vote was larger than had been expected and it effectively rebutted the increasingly shrill claims from White House officials that the impeachment inquiry was a highly partisan "witch hunt" and that the committee amounted to "a kangaroo court." The range of Republican support for impeachment, embracing the Midwest's Harold Froehlich and Tom Railsback, the South's M. Caldwell Butler, the East's Hamilton Fish and New England's William Cohen, may well influence wavering Republicans when the full House acts on the committee's recommendation. The influential roles played in the committee's decision to impeach by its articulate Southern Democrats, Alabama's Walter Flowers, South Carolina's James Mann and Arkansas' Ray Thornton may also swing other Southern congressmen against the President.

Although the committee's final public deliberation sometimes drifted into partisan bickering and time-consuming parliamentary gamesmanship, the result vindicated the patience and pace of the committee's determined chairman Peter Rodino. Through some seven months of laborious study, he kept the committee's overworked staff and its philosophically and temperamentally diverse members driving toward a resolution of its agonizing dilemma. When his committee faced its final act of judgment, the country was treated to a surprise: a group of nationally obscure and generally underrated congressmen and congresswomen rose to the occasion. Often with eloquence and poise, they faced the television cameras and demonstrated their mastery of complex detail, their dedication to duty, and their conscientious search for solutions that would best serve the public interest.

Rodino had long since been thoroughly convinced that impeachment was warranted by the committee's vast accumulation of evidence that was presented by Special Counsel John Doar and Minority Counsel Albert Jenner through eleven weeks of closed hearings and laid out in thirty-six notebooks of "statements of information." Rodino had one main aim as the days of decision approached: to secure maximum committee support for any articles of impeachment that would be recommended to the House. He knew that there was no hope of enlisting about ten Republicans firmly committed to Nixon's defense, but he hoped that articles could be drawn in a way that would attract the remaining Republicans, all troubled by some of Nixon's Watergate-related actions. Yet he also had the problem of not limiting the charges against the President so narrowly that the more liberal Democrats would insist on toughening the language or adding more articles. Rodino was worried too about some of the Southern Democrats, whose home districts tend to favor Nixon heavily.

Rodino and some House Democratic leaders then moved adroitly to seek the help of the Southern Democrats on the committee. These men, Flowers, Mann and Thornton, were offended by Nixon's encroachment on the Constitution and on such agencies as the FBI and IRS. They also are persuasive, soft-sell politicians with an ability to find common cause with the undecided Republicans. The key to gaining maximum support for articles, one House leader explained, was "to put together the Southern Democrats and the Republicans." The way to do that, this veteran told Rodino, was "to get Walter Flowers."

Well aware that his state of Alabama had long liked Nixon, Flowers seemed the most likely Democrat to vote against impeachment. He had developed an ulcer over the problem. Gently, Rodino urged Flowers to seek meetings with the moderate Republicans to see if they might find areas of agreement. The chairman asked the articulate and diplomatic Mann to do the same thing. By Tuesday, private meetings had begun among three Southerners and four uncommitted Republicans: Railsback, Cohen, Butler and

Fish. This centrist group stood between the all-out im-
peachers and the Nixon loyalists.

Another Southern Democrat, Jack Brooks of Texas, also
played a shrewd backstage role as the committee struggled
for consensus. A persistent Nixon critic, Brooks prepared
and distributed to all members of the committee a sweeping series of articles of impeachment that were poorly
drawn and too strong for most of the undecided members.
But the articles had their intended effect; many members
reacted against the Brooks proposals and began working
on alternative drafts of their own. As one staff leader later
explained, "That got the members thinking. They also began to wake up to the fact that they shouldn't leave it to
Doar and the staff."

The general domination of the staff work by Doar was
resented by some veteran committee members. They felt
that their regular counsel, Jerome Zeifman, a forty-nine-
year-old Democratic liberal, had been shunted aside by
Doar, who had been recruited from the outside. Seeking
advice and help from Zeifman, many of the majority Democrats began framing articles of their own as alternatives
to those presented by Doar and those of Brooks. Rodino
purposely refrained from taking part in the drafting sessions but kept in touch with all of them. He saw his role
as a coordinator who would be more effective if he did not
become identified with specific draft proposals.

Soon two overlapping groups were working on articles:
(1) a partial Democratic caucus, heavily influenced by
Brooks but not dominated by him; and (2) the coalition of
Southern Democrats and impeachment-leaning Republicans. The Southerners were able to shuttle between the two
groups and thus were especially influential. Surprisingly,
the coalition group moved more quickly toward agreement
than the all-Democratic drafters. By the end of Tuesday,
said one of the coalition congressmen, "We had unanimity,
a consensus, in two major areas: the abuse of power and
the obstruction of justice." It was then clear that at least

four Republicans—Railsback, Cohen, Butler and Fish—
would go for impeachment.

How Private Decisions Were Made

In this seven-member coalition, the thinking of Southern
Democrat and Northern Republican had much in common.
"I had a yearning, an innate desire to find the President
innocent," recalled Walter Flowers. "I put the blinders on
like the old mule used to wear going down the road with
the wagon behind him. I couldn't see anything ahead except the road." He was particularly troubled by the March
21, 1973, tape, not merely the celebrated "For Christ's sake,
get it" quote, but rather, as Flowers put it, "the matter-of-
fact way in which the payment of hush money was discussed. It shocked my conscience, I'll tell you." He was also
disturbed by the discrepancy between what the President
was doing and what he was saying. "You take the whole
sordid mess and compare it to the public pronouncements
of the President, and it just doesn't fit." He talked often
with Ray Thornton and James Mann, sometimes as they
walked together to the House floor, and finally decided.
"I felt that if we didn't impeach, we'd just ingrain and
stamp in our highest office a standard of conduct that's
just unacceptable."

Flowers in turn was an important influence on the Republicans in the group. At a Sunday meeting, he told the
undecided seven, "This is something we just cannot walk
away from. It happened, and now we've got to deal with it."
Recalled Caldwell Butler later: "I knew at that second he
was right." Butler, whose Virginia district is heavily pro-
Nixon, made his decision soon after a visit to his district by
Vice President Gerald Ford, who assured the voters that he
would support Butler for reelection this fall no matter how
he voted on impeachment.

Suddenly, a fifth Republican, who had remained aloof
from the others and kept his intention quiet, broke away
from Nixon. Lawrence Hogan did so publicly in a harsh

statement against the President that dismayed party loyalists on the committee and undoubtedly had a psychological impact on the undecideds.

> The evidence convinces me that my President has lied repeatedly [Hogan said at a press conference], deceiving public officials and the American people. Instead of cooperating with prosecutors and investigators, as he said publicly, he concealed and covered up evidence, and coached witnesses so that their testimony would show things that really were not true . . . he praised and rewarded those who he knew had committed perjury. He actively participated in an extended and extensive conspiracy to obstruct justice.

A conservative seeking the governorship of Maryland, Hogan frankly conceded that he spoke out early so that his views would not be lost in the committee's thirty-eight-member debate. His later, strong arguments in that debate left little doubt of his sincerity in urging impeachment, even though his act probably was a political plus in Maryland.

Describing how he reached his decision, Hogan recalled that he began listening to the evidence with a "firm presumption" that the President was innocent. "But after reading the transcripts," he said, "it was sobering: the number of untruths, the deception and the immoral attitudes. At that point, I began tilting against the President, and my conviction grew steadily."

While driving home one evening a week ago, he suddenly realized that he had made up his mind to vote for impeachment. "There was just too much evidence," he remarked later. "By any standard of proof demanded, we had to bind him over for trial and removal by the Senate." When he got home, he told his wife of his decision. "She said, 'Good,'" Hogan reported, "the first direct political advice she's ever offered."

The Anguish of Responsibility

On Wednesday, in their private drafting sessions, the two groups of pro-impeachment forces began coalescing.

The Democratic group was reaching agreement on the same two general articles as the coalition negotiators had decided on: obstruction of justice and abuse of power. As the formal opening of the televised Judiciary committee meetings approached, however, the Democratic group had not completed its drafting work. Its members still wondered whether there should be a third article charging Nixon with contempt of Congress for ignoring the committee's subpoenas. Two articles were hastily sketched out, mainly by South Carolina's Mann. "A lot of the real nuts and bolts were put together by Mann," said one participant. The coalition group, also heavily influenced by Mann, had its similar proposals ready. Actually, the unperfected Democratic proposals were the ones later introduced by Harold Donohue of Massachusetts as the takeoff points for the extended debate.

The public moment of truth arrived as Chairman Rodino banged his gavel in the Judiciary committee's draped and paneled room at 7:44 P.M. on Wednesday. Quickly the congressmen and congresswomen dispelled any fears of their Capitol Hill colleagues that they might disgrace the national legislature in this first televised debate and decision of a congressional committee. The tone of solemnity and historic significance was established by the chairman.

Throughout all of the painstaking proceedings of this committee [said Rodino in his thin voice], I as the chairman have been guided by a simple principle, the principle that the law must deal fairly with every man. For me, this is the oldest principle of democracy. It is this simple but great principle which enables man to live justly and in decency in a free society. . . . Make no mistake about it. This is a turning point whatever we decide. Our judgment is not concerned with an individual but with a system of constitutional government. . . . Whatever we now decide, we must have the integrity and the decency, the will and the courage to decide rightly. Let us leave the Constitution as unimpaired for our children as our predecessors left it to us.

In opening statements ranging up to fifteen minutes, the members one after another expressed their individual anguish over the decision they faced. Burdened by the problem of party loyalty, the Republicans suffered most. Declared Cohen: "I have been faced with the terrible responsibility of assessing the conduct of a President that I voted for, believed to be the best man to lead this country, who has made significant and lasting contributions toward securing peace in this country, throughout the world, but a President who in the process by act or acquiescence allowed the rule of law and the Constitution to slip under the boots of indifference and arrogance and abuse."

"How distasteful this proceeding is for me," protested Virginia's assertively fast-talking Butler, explaining that he had worked with Nixon in every one of the President's national elections, "and I would not be here today if it were not for our joint effort in 1972." Wistfully, Illinois' troubled and emotional Railsback sought escape. "I wish the President could do something to absolve himself," he said. Even New Jersey's Charles Sandman abandoned his brawling manner to explain: "For the first time in my life I have to judge a Republican, a man who holds the most powerful office in the world. . . . This is the most important thing I shall ever do in my whole life, and I know it."

To New York Democrat Charles Rangel, the occasion had a positive side. "Some say this is a sad day in America's history," he said. "I think it could perhaps be one of our brightest days. It could be really a test of the strength of our Constitution, because what I think it means to most Americans is that when this or any other President violates his sacred oath of office, the people are not left helpless."

Although some tried to keep their opening statements neutral, most revealed their position on impeachment right off, and at first there were few surprises. Wisconsin's Democrat Robert Kastenmeier contended that "President Nixon's conduct in office is a case history of the abuse of presidential power." New York Democrat Elizabeth Holtzman detected "a seamless web of misconduct so serious that it leaves me shaken." Texan Brooks claimed that the committee evidence traced "government corruption unequaled in the history of the United States." Asked Republican Cohen: "How in the world did we ever get from the Federalist papers to the edited transcripts?"

In the view of many members of the committee's majority, failure to impeach would do far greater harm to the nation's welfare than would the trauma of a Senate trial. Surprising his colleagues with the vehemence of his anti-Nixon stand, Republican Butler declared: "If we fail to impeach, we will have condoned and left unpunished a course of conduct totally inconsistent with the reasonable expectations of the American people . . . and we will have said to the American people, 'These deeds are inconsequential and unimportant.' "

Democrat Thornton claimed that such a failure "would effectively repeal the right of this body to act as a check on the abuses that we see." After breathlessly reeling off a lengthy list of specific improper Nixon acts, Railsback warned of another result. Speaking of the nation's young people, he claimed: "You are going to see the most frustrated people, the most turned-off people, the most disillusioned people, and it is going to make the period of L.B.J. in 1968, 1967 . . . look tame."

The President's Staunchest Defenders

"To become congressmen and congresswomen," noted Missouri Democrat William Hungate, "we took the same oath to uphold the Constitution which Richard M. Nixon took. If we are to be faithful to our oaths, we must find him faithless in his." Iowa Democrat Edward Mezvinsky expressed a similar thought, arguing that Nixon should be brought "to account for the gross abuse of office," and that "we must all ask ourselves, if we do not, who will?"

The President's staunchest defenders quickly proved to be Sandman, California's Charles Wiggins and Indiana's David Dennis. Sandman called the impeachment of President Andrew Johnson in 1868 "one of the darkest moments in the Government of this great nation," and added: "I do not propose to be any part of a second blotch on the history of this great nation."

Nixon's supporters chose mainly to attack the nature of the evidence on which the committee majority had based articles of impeachment. "This case must be decided according to the law, and on no other basis," noted Wiggins. Posing sharp legalistic questions, Wiggins insisted that perhaps only half of one volume among the committee's books of evidence would be admissible in a Senate trial of the President. "Simple theories, of course, are inadequate. That is not evidence. A supposition, however persuasive, is not evidence. A bare possibility that something might have happened is not evidence."

To follow an evidentiary trail from the improper activities of Nixon's aides to the President, argued California Republican Carlos Moorhead, "there is a big moat that you have to jump across to get the President involved—and I cannot jump over that moat." Mississippi Republican Trent Lott argued with vigor that "for every bit of evidence implicating the President, there is evidence to the contrary." The case against Nixon, contended Iowa Republican Wiley Mayne, consists of "a series of inferences piled upon other inferences."

In rapid-fire rebuttal, many of the committee Democrats in their turn rattled off specific presidential acts and conversations, particularly from the President's tapes, that they considered solid evidence. But the most effective general reply was offered by Republican Cohen. "Conspiracies are not born in the sunlight of direct observations," he said. "They are hatched in dark recesses, amid whispers and code words and verbal signals, and many times the footprints of guilt must be traced with a searchlight of probability, of common experience." Moreover, circumstantial evidence is admissible in trials, Cohen noted, and it is often persuasive. He cited as an example that someone who had gone to sleep

at night when the ground was bare and awoke to find snow
on the ground could reasonably conclude that snow had
fallen while he slept.

The Pro-Impeachment Republicans

Some members used their opening statements to make
impassioned pleas for articles of impeachment that seemed
unlikely to win support from a majority of their colleagues.
Father Robert Drinan, a Massachusetts Democrat, argued
that it was wrong not to cite Nixon for the secret bombing
of Cambodia just because it would not "fly" or "play in
Peoria." Asked Drinan: "How can we impeach the President for concealing a burglary but not for concealing a
massive bombing?" Surprisingly, New York Republican
Henry Smith, considered wholly against impeachment, indicated that the Cambodia bombing was the one Nixon offense that he might consider impeachable. Mezvinsky urged
that Nixon be cited for income tax evasion.

Running through Wednesday night and most of Thursday, the opening statements publicly confirmed Republican
defections from the President that had become apparent in
the closed-door strategy sessions on the eve of the debate.
Demonstrating a willingness to impeach on at least one
mainstream article were Illinois' Robert McClory, Railsback, Fish, Butler and Cohen. In a speech that was at first
tantalizingly noncommittal, Froehlich hinted that he might
go along with an article on the obstruction of justice in the
Watergate cover-up.

Hogan followed his previous attack on Nixon with another assault. When Nixon and his aides discussed Watergate burglar E. Howard Hunt's demands for money in the
celebrated March 21, 1973, White House conversation, Hogan protested: "The President didn't, in righteous indig-
nation, rise up and say, 'Get out of here. You are in the
office of the President of the United States. How can you
talk about blackmail and bribery and keeping witnesses
silent?' . . . And then throw them out of his office and pick

up the phone and call the Department of Justice and tell them there is obstruction of justice going on. But my President didn't do that. He sat there, and he worked and worked to try to cover this thing up so it wouldn't come to light."

Most of the pro-impeachment Republicans seemed to feel that the voters would stand by them. Hogan reported that as of last Friday his telephone calls from Marylanders were running 1,072 to 634 in favor of his decision. Butler's early mail ran about 50-50, but he also received vicious and obscene hate calls at his Roanoke home, upsetting his wife June. At week's end Butler requested an unlisted telephone number, but he was not backing down. "If it's come to that," he muttered, "maybe we're impeaching the man too late. My God, these people will have a chance within six months to express their opinion of my performance in office. This type of activity is totally beyond me."

Still not satisfied with the quickly prepared articles of impeachment introduced under Donohue's name, the impeachment forces went to work on new drafts as soon as the round of general debate was concluded on Thursday night. At this critical stage, Chairman Rodino joined the group of key Democrats assembled in Counsel Zeifman's office. Among them were Flowers and Mann, who now held the virtual proxy votes of moderate Republicans. Their aim was to find precisely the right language that would placate the more liberal Democrats, hold the Southerners as well as the available Republicans, and yet be technically proficient enough to withstand the anticipated assault from the Nixon loyalists during the closing debate.

The drafting was resumed Friday morning, delaying the start of that day's public session until 11:55. Finally, with little substantive change but a tightening and polishing of wording, the articles were introduced as an amendment to the Donohue articles by Maryland Democrat Paul Sarbanes, a precise, slow-speaking Rhodes scholar.

Before acting on the amendment, however, the legislators debated two time-consuming diversionary problems in a somewhat quarrelsome and highly repetitive lawyerly argument. At one point, Rodino tried to reduce each member's debating time from five minutes to two minutes, but objections were raised. He then retained his evenhanded treatment of the contending parties, letting the debate drone on.

But if the words were sometimes weak, the images and personalities of the committee were vividly etched on a viewer's consciousness as the proceedings continued. The TV cameras enabled Americans for the first time to see for themselves just how representative this remarkably diverse group of United States Representatives really is. With few exceptions, they seemed less a group of politicians or lawyers (which all are) than a particularly well-cut cross-section of ordinary Americans, exposing the accents, the attitudes, the argot of the regions from which they come, and the universal Chaucerian splay of individual character.

There was Rangel, with big-city bluntness inviting his adversaries "to walk down this street" of evidence with him for a way. There was Thornton, speaking simply and sparingly with the unmistakable sincerity of his Arkansas folk. "It is amazing," Sandman boomed in a kind of McCarthyesque excess of sarcasm and leering, as he hacked at some pro-impeachment speaker's folly. Then came the patient, adenoidal, invariably intelligent queries of Wiggins, forever asking how the evidence touched the President. Or the schoolmasterly, quick thrusts of Dennis, clipping words and arguments.

The Deep Southerners, Flowers and Trent Lott, though on opposite sides, spoke with the easy fluidity and courtesy of their heritage. Mezvinsky was the new boy, carefully following the mood and model of his elders, Cohen the engagingly gawky bright boy of the class. Missouri's Hungate, full of sometimes slightly hokey Ozark folklore, designated himself the comic, just as California's Jerome Waldie attempted wry wit. Texas Democrat Barbara Jordan loomed and boomed like some elemental force, her cultivated accent and erudition surprising each time she spoke. If there seemed a kind of fastidious smirkiness in Delbert Latta, then by contrast Fish and Mayne, Kastenmeier and Mann exuded a quiet and impressive earnestness and integrity. (Kastenmeier displayed probably the most imposing arched eyebrows since John Barrymore's.) For all their differences, the committee members clearly seemed to share the camaraderie of shipmates on an awesome voyage that none had chosen but all must take, to whatever end.

How Specific Must an Article Be?

In the general debate, the first sidetracking stemmed from an attempt by Republican McClory to delay proceedings for ten days if the President would promptly agree to give the House Judiciary committee the same tapes he had been ordered by the Supreme Court to yield to Federal Judge John J. Sirica for use by Special Prosecutor Jaworski in the impending Watergate cover-up trial. Actually, McClory conceded that he had little expectation of a favorable response from Nixon. McClory's tactic was aimed at strengthening a contempt of Congress article against the President he planned to introduce. The motion was defeated 27 to 11 in the first rough test of the committee's voting lineup.

As direct debate on the Sarbanes amendment got under way, the committee fell into a second argument over just how specific or general the articles of impeachment ought to be. The Nixon loyalists, sometimes joined by more moderate Republicans, insisted that the proposed articles were much too vaguely phrased. Democratic defenders of the articles contended that the supporting facts should—and would—be included in the committee's final report and not jammed into the brief impeachment articles. The spirited argument had some light moments. Insisting that inferences can always be drawn from any given fact, Hungate suggested that "if someone brought an elephant through that door and I said 'That's an elephant,' someone would say, 'That's an inference. It could be a mouse with a glandular condition.'" There were sharp personal exchanges as the committee grew restive. Latta irrelevantly criticized Counsel Jenner for having publicly supported the repeal of anti-prostitution legislation, and Latta in turn was scolded by Ohio Democrat John Seiberling for his improper remarks.

The opposing viewpoints on specificity were best expressed by Sandman and Jordan. Growled Sandman: "Why, even a simple parking ticket has to be specific . . . yet you want to replace that [requirement] and say it doesn't apply to the President. Why, that's ridiculous!"

Jordan (referred to as "the gentlelady" by Rodino) noted that the President was not being deprived of any information or due process. His lawyer James St. Clair had been permitted to sit through all the committee hearings on the evidence, receive all the documents given committee members, and cross-examine witnesses. "That was due process," she said. "Due process tripled, due process quadrupled." The Nixon loyalists, she charged, were using "phantom arguments, bottomless arguments."

The proponents of more specific articles had a plausible argument in wishing the charges to be as clear as possible, both out of fairness to the President and a desire to make the task of the House easier in judging the articles. Yet the nature of the charges against the President is not confined to single acts but often embraces a course of conduct over a span of time involving many acts. To be specific would produce lengthy and complex articles. The framers of the articles, moreover, did not want to be confined too strictly to each specific claim, since that would limit the evidence that could eventually be used in the Senate. The specifics would be spelled out in the committee's report.

The long hours consumed in the dispute were turned into a prime-time display of partisan maneuvering. The Nixon supporters sought to delay a final vote, hoping to discredit and discourage the majority, perhaps even win back one or two of their strayed Republicans. Since the loyalists were demanding facts, many Democrats used their turn at the microphones to spin out the litany, as they saw it, of Nixon's misdeeds. Most able of all at this was California's Waldie, whose sporadic running narrative was dismissed by Republican Wiggins as "Waldie's fable."

Sandman moved to strike the first paragraph of the Sarbanes articles and threatened to make the same move against eight other paragraphs. When a vote was finally held late Friday night, Sandman's move was defeated by the same 27 to 11 margin (although there was some shifting of sides in the two votes). That took much of the steam out of a peripheral argument that centered on form rather than substance.

The Facts Behind the Charges

By the next day, Sandman, at least, saw little benefit in pursuing the fight over specificity. "The argument was exhausted yesterday," he conceded to the committee, then withdrew his other eight motions to strike portions of the article under consideration. But now, having been harassed for their failure to detail each general complaint against Nixon, the Democrats were more than ready. They turned the tables, introducing motions to strike paragraphs as a means of debating the facts behind each charge. That was as time-consuming as had been the Republican tactics of the day before, although Democrats argued that the educational value of explaining each charge was worthwhile.

The tactic was led by Flowers, who introduced the strike motion, then yielded his time to sympathetic colleagues. Cohen also took advantage of the situation by securing time to buttress his contention that Nixon had withheld evidence from various Watergate investigators. Sandman protested the reversed situation, complaining that the proceedings were achieving little and boring the viewing public. Nevertheless, some enlightening and sharp ex-

changes of views on facts of evidence were televised throughout Saturday afternoon and into the evening.

Wiggins and Dennis among the Nixon loyalists were
pitted against Democrats George Danielson, Wayne Owens
and Hungate. Every time a vote was taken on Flowers' motions to eliminate paragraphs, the proposals lost decisively;
most of the time Flowers merely responded "Present," not
voting on his own motion. When Sandman found it amazing that Flowers was not voting for his proposals, the Democrat got the laugh of the day by replying, "Well, the cal-
iber of the debate is so outstanding that it leaves me
undecided at the conclusion."

The reality of the debate was that no minds on the
committee were being changed, but the cases for and
against the President were being staked out for the showdown on the floor of the House. Noting the Democratic
lineup against him on the committee, Sandman told fellow
Nixon supporters: "You're going to have a far better forum
on another day—in the House."

Finally all of the amendments were dispensed with and
Chairman Rodino asked for the vote on the articles presented by Sarbanes, as amended slightly, even though all
knew what the general outcome would be; the ensuing tense
roll call was a moving, memorable moment. The only questionable vote was that of Froehlich, who cast a soft "Aye"
that caused a murmur to ripple through the otherwise silent
crowd of fewer than three hundred reporters and spectators.

Several of the congressmen bowed their heads as the
vote was taken. Arkansas' Thornton closed his eyes as if in
prayer. Democrats Seiberling and Mann and Republican
Wiggins appeared close to tears. Almost all the "Ayes" were
delivered in mournful, almost sepulchral tones. By contrast, the first "No"—from Edward Hutchinson—sounded
buoyant and was accompanied by a thin smile.

After the Sarbanes substitute article passed, the final
vote on the article as amended was anticlimactic, even
though it marked the official passage of the first impeach-

ment article against Nixon. "Article I of that resolution of impeachment will be reported to the House," Chairman Rodino announced just before recessing the committee.

This week [August 5, 1974] its deliberations on other proposed articles will begin. An article charging the President with abusing the powers of his office seems likely to pick up the same margin of support, possibly with the addition of Republican McClory. He is also expected to introduce an article of his own, charging Nixon with contempt of Congress for failing to respond to the Judiciary committee's subpoenas. [Subsequently the committee passed two more articles of impeachment, for a total of three. The second article accused Richard Nixon of abusing the powers of his office and failing to take care that the laws be faithfully executed. The third charged him with deliberately disobeying subpoenas from the Judiciary committee for White House tape recordings and documents.—Ed.]

RESIGNATION AND TRANSITION [3]

For more than two years the mystery of Richard M. Nixon's role in Watergate, with all its ramifications and strange twists, had held millions of Americans transfixed. . . . [In the first week of August 1974] in a sudden rush of events, like the final pages of a detective novel, it was all over.

Mr. Nixon, forced to resign as President after publicly admitting his guilt, was in retirement in San Clemente with almost two and a half years remaining in the term to which he had been elected by a landslide. Gerald R. Ford, the man Mr. Nixon had chosen ten months ago to replace a disgraced Vice President, Spiro T. Agnew, was President.

At the beginning of last week [August 5, 1974], the question was whether President Nixon could survive a Senate trial after certain impeachment in the House. At the

[3] From "The Sad, Swift Transition from Nixon to Ford," article by John Herbers, of the New York *Times* Washington Bureau. New York *Times*. p E 1. Ag. 11, '74. © 1974 by The New York Times Company. Reprinted by permission.

end of the week the question was what kind of Government President Ford would bring to a nation torn by long months of uncertainty and division.

Never before had an American President resigned; never before had an unelected official succeeded to the presidency; and only after the death of a President had there been such rapid transition of power. In both major political parties and all across the country there was a sense of sadness over Mr. Nixon's personal fate and over the trauma the nation had undergone. But there was also a clear sense of relief that the inevitable had at last come to pass, that the constitutional system for correcting abuse of power had worked.

And the new President, in his initial words and actions, raised hopes that even though he had long been Mr. Nixon's political ally, he was aware of the erosion of public confidence in government that the Nixon Administration had brought and would seek to repair the damage. "Our great republic is a government of laws and not of men," he said in his address after taking the oath of office. "Here the people rule.". . .

The first hint of crisis came on Sunday when President Nixon called his chief lawyer, James D. St. Clair, his top aides and speechwriters to Camp David, the presidential retreat in Maryland. Even then he was in deep trouble. The House Judiciary committee had voted out three articles of impeachment, and Mr. Nixon had been informed by his aides that the articles would be approved by the full House by a wide margin, and that it was doubtful he could muster the thirty-four votes needed in the Senate to escape conviction and removal from office.

But that was not all. By unanimous order of the Supreme Court, Mr. Nixon had been turning over to Judge John J. Sirica tape recordings of presidential conversations subpoenaed by Special Prosecutor Leon Jaworski for use in the trial next month of some of the Watergate defendants. On one of the tapes, on June 23, 1972, just six days after the burglary and bugging of Democratic headquarters in the Watergate complex, H. R. Haldeman, then the White House chief of staff, told Mr. Nixon that his campaign manager, John N. Mitchell, had consented to the illegal operation. In the course of the conversation, Mr. Nixon ordered that the Federal Bureau of Investigation be told: "Don't go any further into this case."

There was the "smoking pistol" Mr. Nixon's lawyers and his defenders in Congress had argued was missing from the evidence. Even without it, there was growing opinion in Congress that there was a pattern of obstruction of justice by Mr. Nixon in the great body of evidence that the Judiciary committee had assembled, as well as unconstitutional abuse of power of his office. But here was clear evidence under Mr. Nixon's own narrow definition of an impeachable offense—proof of a serious crime committed in the course of his conduct of office was necessary to remove a President.

Further, the June 23 tapes made a lie of Mr. Nixon's public statements, repeated over and over, that he had not learned of the cover-up until March 21, 1973, nine months later, and when he did he moved quickly to see that justice was done. On April 30 . . . [1974], he had released a large volume of edited transcripts of conversations, and he told the American people in a national television address the documents constituted the full story of the President's involvement in Watergate. Yet he had done all he could, short of defying the unanimous Supreme Court, to keep from giving up, through a claim of executive privilege, any of his tapes.

Mr. Nixon's Admission

But all the pertinent existing tapes were going to Judge Sirica for use in a criminal trial and were sure to become known to Congress and the public, most probably before the President's Senate trial. Mr. Nixon had to decide what to do. What he did was difficult to understand but was characteristic of his actions throughout the Watergate case. He made public the transcripts of three June 23 conversations with Haldeman, including the crucial one, and he issued a statement putting his own interpretation on the matter.

He said it was not until sometime last May, after he had released the large volume of transcripts on April, that he listened to the tapes subpoenaed by the court, including those of June 23.

> Although I recognized that these [raised] potential problems, [he said] I did not inform my staff or my counsel of it, or those arguing my case, nor did I amend my submission to the Judiciary committee in order to include and reflect it. At the time, I did not realize the extent of the implications which these conversations might now appear to have. As a result, those arguing my case, as well as those passing judgment on the case, did so with information that was incomplete and in some respects erroneous. This was a serious act of omission for which I take full responsibility.

But he insisted nevertheless that the evidence did not warrant his removal.

It was difficult to believe that a conversation taped just six days after the burglary was not discovered before May of this year. Mr. Nixon and certain of his lawyers and assistants had spent many hours over the tapes long before May. Mr. St. Clair, the Boston lawyer who joined the staff last January, apparently was surprised and angered and was reported to have insisted on the President's admission that he kept the information from his lawyers. Yet what had gone on in the dark labyrinths of the Nixon White House now seemed unimportant as the attrition of political support for the President became an avalanche.

"I feel I have been deceived," said Representative Edward Hutchinson of Michigan, the ranking Republican on the House Judiciary committee. So did the other ten members of the committee who had put their reputations on the line and defended Mr. Nixon for five days on national television. And it was the same throughout Congress. Mr.

Nixon had conceded his impeachment even before the release of the new evidence. Now his conviction in the Senate and removal became a certainty. And it was his political friends, acting out of a sense of betrayal, not the liberal Democrats he had accused of conducting a political vendetta against him, who did it.

Still, Mr. Nixon did not give up until the full dimension of the landslide was evident. On Tuesday he called a Cabinet meeting and said he would let the full constitutional process of impeachment and removal run its course, because he did not believe he had committed an impeachable offense. The crisis built. The stock market rose as predictions of impeachment swamped the nation, then declined when Mr. Nixon said he was holding on. Crowds gathered outside the White House for the first time since the Saturday Night Massacre of last October [1973], when Mr. Nixon fired Special Prosecutor Archibald Cox and gave the impeachment inquiry legitimacy and drive.

Prosecution Remains Possible

He confessed to being deeply hurt by his removal. He had wanted very much, he told associates, to be President when the nation celebrates its two hundredth anniversary in 1976. But that may now be the least of his agony. He left office with no apparent assurances against being prosecuted for the Watergate crimes. Special Prosecutor Leon Jaworski said he had made no agreement for immunity, and indeed he may have a legal obligation to bring charges. Mr. Nixon was named by a Watergate grand jury as an unindicted coconspirator in the Watergate cover-up, a citation that would have been an indictment had Mr. Nixon not been President. And that was without the evidence on the June 23, 1972, tapes.

Thus Mr. Nixon, out of office as in, left the nation to wrestle with a moral problem—should a former President be excused from prosecution on the ground that his removal constituted substantial punishment, or should he be treated like any other citizen under the law? The Constitution clearly states that his removal should not be a bar to later criminal prosecution.

The sixty-one-year-old man from Whittier, California, left behind one of the strangest chapters in American history, a two-year drama and trauma that constituted not only the deepest corruption of any American presidency but a constant mystery with one central question: How deeply was the President involved?

Yet one of the ironies was that it did not keep Richard Nixon from winning a second term in 1972 with more than 60 percent of the vote. The White House, with its enormous power to both control the agencies of Government and influence public opinion, managed through the election to make it appear to most Americans that only a few low-grade employees of the President's reelection committee had anything to do with the burglary and the bugging.

It was not until early in 1973 that the complexity of White House involvement was disclosed. The special Senate Watergate committee headed by Sam J. Ervin, Democrat of North Carolina, learned of the existence of tape recordings and the involvement of the President's chief aides.

Then followed the Saturday Night Massacre; the startling disclosure that an eighteen-and-one-half-minute portion of a crucial conversation by the President had been erased; reports of other scandals, including Mr. Nixon's underpayment of income taxes of more than $400,000; impeachment proceedings by a reluctant Congress; the climactic, televised proceedings of the House Judiciary committee; the Supreme Court decision on the case that helped make a vote to impeach the President respectable; and then the swift ending last week.

The plain man from Grand Rapids, Michigan, became the thirty-eighth President in a simple swearing-in ceremony in the East Room at noon on Thursday. In his brief address afterwards he said, "My fellow Americans, our long national nightmare is over. Our Constitution works."

THE CONSTITUTION WORKS [4]

We have had constitutional crises before but, except for the Civil War and Reconstruction, none that had the dimensions of those precipitated by Richard M. Nixon. Never before have we had a crisis that challenged the basic assumptions of our constitutional system itself, and the basic processes and mechanisms through which it worked.

Alexander Hamilton, though he supported the Constitution, thought it "a frail and worthless fabric" and had no confidence that it would endure. And no wonder. It was, after all, without precedent or model in history. Never before had a people made a national Constitution; never before had they fabricated a federal system; never before had they elected a national head of state; never before had they fixed effective limits on government by such devices as a genuine separation of powers, and bills of substantive rights, that had the force of law.

Almost miraculously the system worked. The "frail and worthless fabric" proved to be both tough and enduring and, what is more astonishing, proved wonderfully resilient. Under its auspices the United States grew from thirteen to fifty states; under its auspices it weathered one crisis after another, and that without suspending any of its great provisions, without impairing the authority and dignity of the presidency, the power of the Congress or the independence of the Judiciary.

In 1861 the South challenged the Constitution, and set up on its own; then it honored the document by transforming it, with only minor changes, into a constitution for the Confederacy.

The Constitution survived the First World War, the crisis of the great Depression and the challenge of the wel-

[4] From "The Constitution Is Alive and Well," article by Henry Steele Commager, professor of history at Amherst College. New York *Times*. p E 17. Ag. 11, '74. © 1974 by the New York Times Company. Reprinted by permission.

fare state, and the unprecedented strains of the Second
World War.

One reason the Constitution survived intact was that no
President had ever attempted to subvert it, no politicians—
with the exception of Aaron Burr—have even threatened it.

Notwithstanding the absence of any tradition of loyalty
to the new Government, the United States, even in infancy,
did not have a Cromwell, nor, in maturity, a Hitler.

Here—for perhaps the first time in modern history—it
was not necessary to call upon loyalty to a king to preserve
the commonwealth.

As Tom Paine put it, "Where then is the King of
America? Know that in America the Constitution is King."

Or as Thomas Jefferson wrote, after he and Hamilton
had frustrated Burr's attempt to steal the election of 1800:

> The tough sides of our Argosy had been thoroughly tried.
> Her strength has stood the waves into which she was steered, with
> a view to sink her. We shall put her on her republican tack and
> she will show by the beauty of her motion, the skill of her
> builders.

For the first time since 1861, an Administration, Mr.
Nixon's, called into question both the beauty of her motion
and the skill of her builders. For what is it that has been at
stake for the last two years—what but the integrity and the
vitality of the Constitution itself and of the principles it
is designed to secure—a more perfect union, justice, domestic tranquillity, and the blessings of liberty, and the rule
of law.

Let us be more specific.

First. The principle of a government of laws and not of
men, a principle so precious that the Founding Fathers
wrote it into many of the state constitutions. By counte-
nancing burglary, wiretapping, *agents provocateurs,* the use
of the Federal Bureau of Investigation, Central Intelligence
Agency and even the Internal Revenue Service to punish
"enemies," by endorsing the Huston plan for the creation

of a police state, and by resort to secrecy, duplicity and deception in the operations of Government, Mr. Nixon sought to substitute his own fiat for the law.

Second. The principle, vindicated by the United States Supreme Court in the great case of *ex parte* Milligan:

> The Constitution is a law for rulers and people, equally in war and in peace, and covers with the shield of its protection all classes of men at all times and under all circumstances. No doctrine involving more pernicious consequences was ever invented by the wit of man than that any of its great provisions can be suspended during any of the great exigencies of government.

By creating sham "exigencies" involving "national security," Mr. Nixon sought to justify the violation of constitutional guarantees of due process and of the fundamental rights of citizens, and of the welfare of society, and authorized withholding of evidence essential to justice—in effect suspending vital provisions of the Constitution.

Third. The principle of the separation of powers, a principle established first by Americans as the most effective method of holding each branch of Government within the framework of the Constitution.

By usurping congressional power to declare war, making war on neutral Cambodia and concealing that war from the Congress and the American people; by shrouding much of the conduct of foreign affairs in a fog of secrecy, denying to the Congress information essential to the faithful performance of its constitutional duties; and by nullifying congressional power over appropriations through the device of impounding funds duly voted by the Congress, Mr. Nixon undermined the integrity of this great principle.

Fourth. The principles of freedom and justice in the Bill of Rights.

By attempting to impose, for the first time in our history, prior censorship of the press, by threatening hostile television stations with deprivation of their licenses, by directing the arrest without warrants of some twelve thousand men and women gathered in the capital city to exercise their constitutional rights of assembly and petition, by flouting the constitutional prohibition against unreasonable search and seizure and the requirement of search warrants, by ignoring the provisions for due process of law in the endorsement of the Huston Plan [see "The List of Potential Charges," in Section I, above] and in the illegal use of the Central Intelligence Agency in domestic affairs, Mr. Nixon presented the most dangerous threat to the Bill of Rights in the whole of our history.

Fifth. The integrity and survival of democratic government in the United States.

By corrupting presidential elections through the solicitation of illegal contributions, by a systematic campaign of mendacity, trickery and character assassination against opponents, by violating the integrity of the civil service and corrupting his closest subordinates, Mr. Nixon gravely endangered the integrity of our republican system of government.

Mr. Nixon's resignation is no voluntary act. It was not inspired by contrition or by a belated loyalty to the Constitution. It was forced on him by a ground swell of public outrage, by a popular ralliance to the Constitution comparable to that which swept the North at the time of Fort Sumter, and by a Congress that after long vacillation finally responded to the standards of duty and the obligations of the Constitution.

The long-drawn-out process of inquiry by committee, by the courts, by the Congress is a stunning vindication of our constitution system, a vindication of the principle of separation of powers, of the independence of the courts and of the foresight of the framers.

The men who made our Constitution were familiar with the history of executive tyranny. They were steeped in the history of the ancient world and knew well the story of usurpation of power, revolution and assassination in the city-states of Greece and in Rome.

They knew, too, the tragic history of England and the fate of a Richard II, a Mary Queen of Scots and a Charles I; they had themselves just fought a war against what they thought to be the tyranny of George III. They were determined to write a new page in history, and did. They accepted the necessity of change in government and in leadership. They invented the great institution of the constitutional convention—a legal way to alter and abolish government and institute new government.

They took over the English practice of impeachment, applied it to their highest office, providing a legal and peaceful method of removing the President himself from office.

Thus, in the words of Alexander Hamilton, they "substituted the mild magistracy of the law for the terrible weapon of the sword."

Confronted, for the first time in our long history, with a chief magistrate who betrayed his oath of office, we have resorted to that "magistracy of the law" and vindicated once again the wisdom of the Founding Fathers. Thus, we have demonstrated to the world and, let us hope, to future generations that the Constitution is alive and well, that it can be adapted to the exigencies of governance, and that in an emergency an enlightened and determined democracy can protect and defend its principles, its honor, and its heritage.

When, on September 17, 1787, members of the Federal Convention came forward to sign the Constitution that they had drafted during those long hot months in Philadelphia, the venerable Dr. Franklin arose and

looking toward the president's chair, at the back of which a rising sun happened to be painted, observed that painters had found it difficult to distinguish in their art between a rising and a setting sun. "I have often and often," said he, "in the

course of the session and the vicissitudes of my hopes and fears
as to its issue looked at that behind the presidency, without
being able to tell whether it was rising or setting. Now at length
I have the happiness to know that it is a rising and not a setting sun."

BIBLIOGRAPHY

An asterisk (*) preceding a reference indicates that the article or a part of it has been reprinted in this book.

BOOKS, PAMPHLETS, AND DOCUMENTS

Barnes, J. M. Presidential government: the crucible of leadership. Houghton. '66.

Berger, Raoul. Executive privilege: a constitutional myth. Harvard University Press. '74.

Berger, Raoul. Impeachment: the constitutional problems. Harvard University Press. '73.

Bernstein, Carl and Woodward, Bob. All the President's men. Simon & Schuster. '74.

Binkley, W. E. The powers of the President. Russell & Russell. '73.

Black, C. L. Jr. Impeachment: a handbook. Yale University Press. '74.

*Bowman, Elizabeth. HEW impoundments. Congressional Quarterly, Inc. '73.
> Excerpt. Christian Science Monitor. p 4. S. 17, '73. Courts erode Nixon policy of impounding money.

Brownson, O. A. The American republic: its constitution, tendencies, and destiny. College & University Press. '72.
> Original edition, 1865.

Burgess, J. W. Recent changes in American constitutional theory. Arno Press. '72.

Burns, J. M. Presidential government: the crucible of leadership. Houghton. '73.

Chester, Lewis and others. Watergate: the full inside story. Ballantine. '73.

Congressional Quarterly. Watergate: chronology of a crisis. Congressional Quarterly. '73.

Corwin, E. S. The President, office and powers, 1787-1957. 4th rev. ed. New York University Press. '57.

Cunliffe, Marcus. American Presidents and the presidency. Eyre Spottiswoode. '69.

Gardner, L. C. comp. The great Nixon turnaround. New Viewpoints. '73.

Hamilton, W. H. and Adair, Douglass. The power to govern. Da Capo Press. '72.

Hughes, E. J. The living presidency: the resources and dilemmas of the American presidential office. Coward, McCann & Geohegan. '73.

Javits, J. K. and Kellermann, Don. Who makes the war; the President versus Congress. Morrow. '73.

Knappman, E. W. and others, eds. Watergate and the White House, June 1972-July 1973. Facts on File. '73.

Laski, H. J. The American presidency. Greenwood Press. '72.
Reprint of 1940 edition.

Lurie, Leonard. The impeachment of Richard Nixon. Berkley. '73.

Mankiewicz, F. F. Perfectly clear: Nixon from Whittier to Watergate. Quadrangle/New York Times Book Company. '73.

Myers, R. J. The tragedies of King Richard. Acropolis Books. '73.

Reedy, G. E. The twilight of the presidency. World Publishing. '70.

Rossiter, C. L. The American presidency. 2d ed. Harcourt, Brace. '60.

Schlesinger, Arthur, Jr. The imperial presidency. Houghton. '73.

Sorenson, T. C. Decision-making in the White House. Columbia University Press. '63.

United States. Congress. Senate. Select Committee on Presidential Campaign Activities. Presidential campaign activities of 1972, Senate resolution 60; Watergate and related activities, phase I: Watergate investigation, hearings. (93d Congress, 1st session) U.S. Gov. Ptg. Office. Washington, D.C. 20401. '73.

——The presidential transcripts, with commentary by the staff of the Washington *Post*. Delacorte. '74.

——The Watergate hearings: break-in and cover-up; proceedings of the Senate Select Committee on Presidential Campaign Activities; as ed. by the staff of the New York *Times*. Bantam Books. '73.

Watergate: the view from the left. Pathfinder Press. '73.

White, T. H. The making of the President 1972. Atheneum. '73.
Excerpt. Reader's Digest. 103:102-9. N. '73. Watergate in perspective.

Woodstone, Arthur. Nixon's head. St. Martins. '72.

<h2>PERIODICALS</h2>

America. 129:319. N. 3, '73. Government of laws or men? Decision to hand over Watergate tapes.

America. 129:366. N. 17, '73. Storm over the White House; question of resignation.

America. 130:182-3. Mr. 16, '74. Politics, morality and impeachment.

American Heritage. 25:22-3+. D. '73. Impoundment. A. L. Damon.

American Heritage. 25:12-15+. F. '74. Veto: a look at the record. A. L. Damon.

American Scholar. 43:21-37. Winter '73. Silent complicity at Watergate. H. F. Stein.

American Scholar. 43:248+. Spring '74. Position paper for the American realist. G. W. Johnson.

American Scholar. 43:249-59. Spring '74. Public morality; afterthoughts on Watergate. Vermont Royster.

Atlantic. 231:45-54. Ap. '73. The First Amendment on trial. Charles Rembar.

Atlantic. 231:55-64. Ap. '73. The President and the press. David Wise.

Atlantic. 232:43-55. N. '73. Runaway presidency. Arthur Schlesinger, Jr.

Atlantic. 233:29-34. Ja. '74. Undoing of the Justice department. S. J. Ungar.

Atlantic. 233:24-5. Mr. '74. Sick of Dick. L. E. Sissman.

Atlantic. 233:56-60+. Ap. '74. Who's running the country? Joseph Kraft.

Atlantic. 233:83-92+. Ap. '74. Judge who tried harder. G. V. Higgins.

*Brookings Bulletin. 10:7-11. Fall '73. Needed: a workable check on the presidency. J. L. Sundquist.

Business Week. p 33-4. O. 20, '73. Triple threat to illegal givers.

*Center Magazine. p 8+. Ja./F. '74. The separation of powers.

Center Magazine. p 9-43. Mr./Ap. '74. Watergate: the constitutional issues.

Christian Century. 90:555-6. My. 16, '73. On seeing the presidency as sacred.

Christian Century. 90:1043-4. O. 24. '73. Agnew case and Christian realism.

Christian Century. 90:1272-5. D. 26, '73. Watergate year as watershed year. M. E. Marty.

Christian Century. 91:87. Ja. 23, '74. Presidential parsimony. M. E. Marty.

*Christian Science Monitor. p 7. Ja. 4, '73. Courts, Congress test Nixon refusal to spend.

*Christian Science Monitor. p 1+. D. 17, '73. Simon: we must act fast.

*Christian Science Monitor. p 8. D. 21, '73. Nixon to continue impounding funds.

Commentary. 57:19-25. Ja. '74. Watergate and the legal order. A. M. Bickel.

Commonweal. 99:286. D. 14, '73. Rx for Richard Nixon. H. J. Gans.

Commonweal. 99:379-80. Ja. 18, '74. Non-government & resignation.

Commonweal. 100:103-6. Ap. 5, '74. Europeanization of American politics. I. L. Horowitz.

*Congressional Quarterly Almanac. 29:776-7. '73. Executive privilege.

*Congressional Quarterly Almanac. 29:777. '73. Kleindienst hearings.

*Congressional Quarterly Almanac. 29:778-9. '73. National emergency powers.

Congressional Quarterly Weekly Report. 36:2395-7. S. 8, '73. Impoundment: Administration loses most court tests.

Current. 155:3-29. O. '73. Meaning of Watergate; symposium.

Current. 159:3-11. F. '74. Is Nixon a foreign policy problem? T. L. Hughes.

Department of State Bulletin. 69:662-4. N. 26, '73. President Nixon's veto of war powers measure overridden by the Congress; text of message and White House statement, October 24 and November 7, 1973. R. M. Nixon.

*Editorial Research Reports. v 1, no 9:167-84. Mr. 7, '73. Presidential accountability. H. B. Shaffer.

Editorial Research Reports. v 2 no 10:691-708. S. 12, '73. Separation of powers. H. B. Shaffer.

*Editorial Research Reports. v 2, no 21:925-46. D. 5, '73. Presidential impeachment. Mary Costello.

Fortune. 89:74-6+. Ja. '74. President-less government in Washington. Lewis Beman.

Nation. 217:419-20. O. 29, '73. Agnew's apologia.

*Nation. 217:514-15. N. 19, '73. Clamor for resignation [editorial].

Nation. 217:562-4. N. 26, '73. Enemy in Orange County: getting the goods on San Clemente.

Nation. 217:610-12. D. 10, '73. Many questions remain; failure of Operation Candor.

Nation. 217:612. D. 10, '73. Historic moment: Senate's confirmation of Gerald Ford.

Nation. 218:130-1. F. 2, '74. Animals in the forest.

Nation. 218:174-9. F. 9, '74. Roots of Watergate. A. I. Waskow.

Nation. 218:194-6. F. 16, '74. Watergate postscript; State of the Union message.

Nation. 218:290-1. Mr. 9, '74. Message from Michigan.

Nation. 218:322. Mr. 16, '74. Continuing conspiracy.

Nation. 218:355. Mr. 23, '74. Ultimate embarrassment.

*National Observer. p 8. Mr. 24, '73. Nixon text on executive privilege.

*National Observer. p 2. Jl. 28, '73. New moves to curb war powers.

National Observer. p 5. F. 9, '74. Nixon's program: a shield against impeachment?

*National Observer. p 2. Mr. 2, '74. House committee debates an "impeachable offense."

National Review. 25:1394+. D. 21, '73. Canto 476: Rose Mary Woods.

National Review. 25:1400. D. 21, '73. Goal line stand; Nixon's battle to hold public opinion. G. F. Will.

National Review. 26:190. F. 15, '74. Capitol issues; newspaper coverage of Watergate. G. F. Will.

National Review. 26:253-5. Mr. 1, '74. Presidency goes nowhere. J. J. Kilpatrick.

National Review. 26:276. Mr. 1, '74. Nixon and resignation. W. F. Buckley, Jr.

National Review. 26:298. Mr. 15, '74. Scope of the disaster.

National Review. 26:364. Mr. 29, '74. In like a lion. G. F. Will.

Nation's Business. 62:11-12. F. '74. Uses of adversity. J. J. Kilpatrick.

New Republic. 169:5-7. N. 3, '73. Impeachment and the House.

New Republic. 169:7-8. N. 10, '73. ITT again; White House involvement in anti-trust suit.

New Republic. 169:19-21. D. 29, '73. CIA and the plumbers. Tad Szulc.

New Republic. 170:5-7. Ja. 19, '74. Moving in on Mr. Nixon.

New Republic. 170:5-6. F. 9, '74. Getting on with impeachment.

New Republic. 170:7-11. F. 16, '74. Billion $ question.

New Republic. 170:5-8. Mr. 16, '74. Impeachment of Mr. Nixon.

New Republic. 170:7. Mr. 30, '74. Televised impeachment?

New York. 6:38+. D. 24, '73. Man who could push Richard Nixon over the edge.

New York Times. p E 1. Ja. 27, '73. The President says, "I'm going to fight like hell."

*New York Times. p E 2. Mr. 18, '73. Executive privilege; a basic power collision. John Herbers.

New York Times. p 41. Ap. 9, '73. Congress's law rating.

New York Times. p E 2. Ap. 15, '73. Presidential secrets; keeping Congress at bay.

*New York Times. p 1+. My. 5, '73. Nixon's imprint is deep at regulatory agencies.

New York Times. p E 1. Jl. 29, '73. Judges' turn.

New York Times. p 12. Jl. 29, '73. The cloud of Watergate [editorial].

New York Times. p E 1. S. 2, '73. Sirica says: Give me the tapes.

New York Times. p E 12. S. 2, '73. Presidential power [editorial].

New York Times. p 1+. O. 13, '73. Appeals Court agrees President should give up tapes.

New York Times. p E 12. O. 14, '73. President or sovereign? [editorial]

New York Times. p 30. O. 22, '73. One-man law . . . [editorial].

New York Times. p 1+. O. 24, '73. Nixon agrees to give tapes to Sirica in compliance with orders of court.

*New York Times. p E 1. O. 28, '73. Suddenly, impeachment is the big, open issue. J. M. Naughton.

New York Times. p 28. O. 31, '73. The prosecutor issue.

*New York Times. p 46. N. 8, '73. A balance regained [editorial].

New York Times. p E 2. N. 11, '73. Confronting the demands, he says, "I won't quit."

New York Times. p E 2. N. 25, '73. The President's problem.

New York Times. p 42. N. 30, '73. Articles of impeachment [editorial].

New York Times. p 39. D. 3, '73. A dangerous law.

New York Times. p 37. Ja. 23, '74. Don't count Nixon out. James Reston.

*New York Times. p 1+. F. 7, '74. House, 410-4, gives subpoena power in Nixon inquiry.

*New York Times. p E 1. F. 10, '74. A catalogue of matters involving the President. D. E. Rosenbaum.

New York Times. p 1+. F. 26, '74. Nixon asserts a criminal offense is required for an impeachment.

New York Times. p B 37. Mr. 10, '74. Big impeachment inquiry staff is quietly writing U.S. history.

New York Times. p 36. Mr. 19, '74. Lions of liberty [editorial].

*New York Times. p E 1. Ag. 11, '74. The sad, swift transition from Nixon to Ford. John Herbers.

*New York Times. p E 17. Ag. 11, '74. The Constitution is alive and well. H. S. Commager.

New York Times Magazine. p 10-11+. Jl. 1, '73. Is America burning? J. A. Michener.

New York Times Magazine. p 7+. Jl. 8, '73. Richard Nixon's seventh crisis. Garry Wills.

New York Times Magazine. p 1+. Jl. 22, '73. Watergate: the story so far. J. A. Lukas.

New York Times Magazine. p 18-19+. S. 23, '73. Why Congress won't fight. Elizabeth Drew.

New York Times Magazine. p 38-9+. O. 14, '73. Constraining of the President. R. E. Neustadt.

New York Times Magazine. p 38-9. N. 11, '73. Who's what around the White House. William Safire.

New York Times Magazine. p 1. Ja. 13, '74. Watergate: the story continued. J. A. Lukas.

New York Times Magazine. p 11-17+. Ja. 13, '74. Money, money, money.

New York Times Magazine. p 32-4+. Ja. 13, '74. Cox and his army.

New York Times Magazine. p 16-17+. Mr. 3, '74. The other presidency.

*New York Times Magazine. p 4. Ap. 7, '74. The mediums [President as news]. Russell Baker.

New Yorker. 49:29. F. 11, '74. Notes and comment.

New Yorker. 49:97-9. F. 4; 50:90-4. Mr. 4; 111-14+. Ap. 1, '74. Letter from Washington. R. H. Rovere.

New Yorker. 50:42-8+. Mr. 11; 41-54+. Mr. 18, '74. Reporter in Washington, D.C.; autumn notes. E. B. Drew.

Newsweek. 81:49-50. My. 14, '73. How the world looks at Watergate.

*Newsweek. 81:60. My. 21, '73. Deep-diggers rampant.

Newsweek. 82:22-6+. O. 29, '73. Great tapes crisis; firing of Archibald Cox.

Newsweek. 82:20-5+. N. 5, '73. Can Nixon survive?

*Newsweek. 82:15. N. 12, '73. Rethinking the Constitution. Morton Mintz.

Newsweek. 82:29-30+. N. 12, '73. Instant replay, the ITT case.

Newsweek. 82:35-9. N. 19, '73. Now, it's Operation Candor.

Newsweek. 82:24-8+. N. 26, '73. Mr. Nixon comes out fighting.

Newsweek. 83:12-13. Ja. 7, '74. Impeachment now? Impeachment eventually? J. K. Galbraith.

Newsweek. 83:16-17. Ja. 7, '74. From Candor to San Clemente.

Newsweek. 83:29-30. Ja. 21, '74. Advocates.

Newsweek. 83:14-17. F. 4, '74. I'm going to fight like hell: Operation Counterattack.

Newsweek. 83:16-19. Mr. 4, '74. Vote of no confidence.

Newsweek. 83:17. Mr. 11, '74. Jury points a finger at Nixon.

Newsweek. 83:23-4+. Mr. 11, '74. Story of the big cover-up.

Newsweek. 83:22-4+. Mr. 25, '74. Operation Friendly Persuasion.

Newsweek. 83:28-30+. Mr. 25, '74. All about impeachment.

*Newsweek. 83:17+. My. 13, '74. A desperate gamble for survival.

*Newsweek. 84:23-6. Ag. 5, '74. A very definitive decision.

Ramparts. 12:12-17+. N. '73. From Dallas to Watergate: the longest cover-up. P. D. Scott.

Reader's Digest. 104:92-8. Ja. '74. Decline and fall of a Vice President.

*Senior Scholastic. 103:4-9. O. 18, '73. Watergate . . . so what.

Senior Scholastic. 103:6-9. N. 1, '73. Who runs the republic: the Congress, or the President?

Senior Scholastic. 103:19. N. 1, '73. Agnew resigns: a tragic day in history.

Senior Scholastic. 103:12-13. N. 8, '73. Did the press hatchet the President on Watergate? [excerpts from interview] John Chancellor.

Senior Scholastic. 103:23. D. 13, '73. President's war powers checked.

Senior Scholastic. 104:23. Mr. 28, '74. Senate panel ends public hearings on Watergate.

Senior Scholastic. 104:17. Ap. 4, '74. To impeach or not to impeach.

Time. 101:82. My. 7, '73. Watergate three; coverage of the Watergate case.

Time. 102:6-13. Jl. 9, '73. Dean's case against the President.

*Time. 102:16-18. Ag. 20, '73. Watergate I: the evidence to date.

Time. 102:16-18. O. 22, '73. The vice presidency: a good lineman for the quarterback.

Time. 102:23-4+. N. 5, '73. Where the Cox probe left off.

Time. 102:20-1. N. 12, '73. The President should resign [editorial].

Time. 102:22-3. N. 12, '73. Mystery of the missing tapes.

Time. 102:45-6. N. 12, '73. Stand-up Texan for a tough task: Leon Jaworski.

Time. 102:30. N. 19, '73. Limiting the power to wage war.

Time. 102:15-18. D. 10, '73. Secretary and the tapes tangle.

Time. 102:24. D. 10, '73. Fuse burns ever closer: admission of guilt by E. Krogh.

Time: 102:78. D. 17, '73. God and Watergate; reactions of churchmen.

Time. 102:12. D. 31, '73. Who owns the President's papers?

*Time. 103:8-15+. Ja. 7, '74. Judge John J. Sirica: standing firm for the primacy of law.

Time. 103:13-18. Ja. 28, '74. Telltale tape deepens Nixon's dilemma.

Time. 103:30-1. F. 4, '74. Facing up to resignation or impeachment.

Time. 103:10-14+. Mr. 11, '74. Seven charged, a report and a briefcase.

Time. 103:17. Mr. 18, '74. Cleaning up campaigns; reform of U.S. campaign laws.

Time. 103:11-14+. Mr. 25, '74. President's strategy for survival.

Time. 103:15-16. Ap. 1, '74. Slipping anchor on the right; conservative support of Richard Nixon.

*Time. 104:10-18. Ag. 5, '74. The fateful vote to impeach.

Today's Education. 63:20-2. Ja.-F. '74. Truth in government. Norman Cousins.

U.S. News & World Report. 75:18. Jl. 30, '73. Executive privilege; what the argument is all about.

U.S. News & World Report. 75:22. O. 8, '73. Turning the case over to a grand jury; statement, September 25, 1973. E. L. Richardson.

U.S. News & World Report. 75:19-21. N. 5, '73. After surrendering tapes, new pressures on Nixon.

U.S. News & World Report. 75:64-5. N. 5, '73. Elliot Richardson tells his side of the story; excerpts from news conference, October 23, 1973.

U.S. News & World Report. 75:70-1. N. 5, '73. From the official record: Nixon's history-making moves; text of Nixon statement of October 19, 1973.

U.S. News & World Report. 75:91. N. 19, '73. How President's war powers are cut; with excerpts from the war powers resolution of 1973.

U.S. News & World Report. 75:27-8. N. 26, '73. Nixon's all-out drive to restore confidence.

U.S. News & World Report. 75:78-82. D. 3, '73. Watergate's impact on future as political scientists see it; nationwide survey.

U.S. News & World Report. 75:26. D. 31, '73. Some Republicans want Nixon to quit [excerpts from interview]. Barry Goldwater.

U.S. News & World Report. 76:22-3. Ja. 7, '74. Nixon vs. Congress: round 6 will be the toughest yet.

U.S. News & World Report. 76:24. F. 11, '74. Watergate, more pressure on President: Nixon subpoenaed in White House aides' trial.

U.S. News & World Report. 76:27-9. Mr. 4, '74. Who's in charge at the White House.

U.S. News & World Report. 76:29. Mr. 4, '74. When the agonizing ended for Nixon.

*U.S. News & World Report. 76:21-4. Mr. 11, '74. Charges against White House.

U.S. News & World Report. 76:20. Mr. 18, '74. President's own explanation of Watergate hush money; excerpt from televised news conference, March 6, 1974.

U.S. News & World Report. 76:24-5. Mr. 25, '74. Role of lawyers in Watergate.

U.S. News & World Report. 76:23-4. Ap. 1, '74. Nixon's big push to head off impeachment.

U.S. News & World Report. 76:24. Ap. 1, '74. Who's who on House's impeachment committee.

U.S. News & World Report. 76:26-7. Ap. 8, '74. White House concession heads off showdown.

*U.S. News & World Report. 76:28-30. Ap. 8, '74. Answers to questions on impeachment.

Vital Speeches of the Day. 40:245-7. F. 1, '74. The President: leader of Western civilization; address, December 15, 1973. F. B. Dent.

Vital Speeches of the Day. 40:364-7. Ap. 1, '74. Historical opportunity for government reforms; address, February 21, 1974. F. H. Hyde.

Wall Street Journal. p 24. My. 15, '73. Cambodia and Congress [editorial].

Wall Street Journal. p 2. Je. 26, '73. Nixon ordered Watergate cover-up but didn't grasp impact, Dean says.

*Wall Street Journal. p 10. Jl. 19, '73. The presidency and the law. Arthur Schlesinger, Jr.

Wall Street Journal. p 16. Jl. 24, '73. On course for crisis [editorial].

Wall Street Journal. p 1+. Ag. 3, '73. Treading softly: Senate and House move to reassert authority but may lose initiative.

Wall Street Journal. p 1+. Ag. 9, '73. Watergate: Act I; as hearings recess, the central question remains unanswered.

Washington Post. p 1+. O. 8, '73. Congress overrides veto, enacts war curbs. R. L. Lyons.

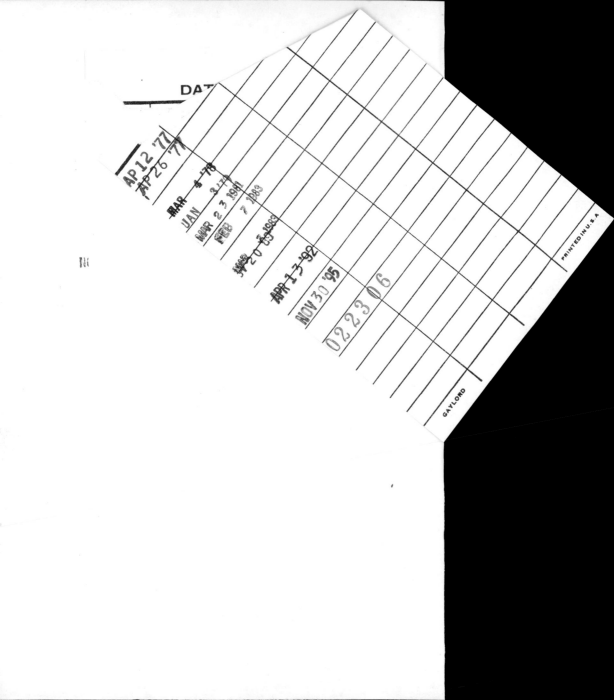